A Heart
Held
Ransomed

"He watched helplessly as everything he held dear to him was snatched away, now he is fighting to expose the dangers of "repressed memories

Written by Stephan Skotko
Co-authored by Teila Tankersley

All chapters written by Stephan Skotko unless
otherwise noted at the chapter head.

Table of Contents

Introduction

A Heart Held Ransomed is a true story, which is so bizarre - you've got to read it to believe it.

Steve Skotko and his wife were the typical American family, and as with most marriages, they had their share of ups and downs so it sounded like a logical decision when Steve and his beautiful wife of twenty six years sought the counsel of a marriage therapist. They did not know they were about to enter the nightmare of their lives. They entered a living hell, which has cost them their family.

Up until this point the Skotko's were unfamiliar with repressed memory therapy. This was until the day their "new" therapist made the accusation the family had all been individually abused when they were children and those memories had been repressed deep inside their subconscious mind.

This new therapist said he was there to help merge those memories back into consciousness. Steve scoffed, but he and his family went to a few more sessions before Steve finally called it quits. The counseling sessions were getting more and more bizarre. Finally, Steve told the counselor they would not be returning. This is when the saga begins; Steve's wife and children continued therapy behind his back, participating in mystical and theatrical counseling sessions.

Repressed memory therapy is very controversial and more and more psychologists now believe without established standards or procedures, a psychotherapist can actually implant false memories into a patients mind. Steve's family was just one of the many millions of victims, which have entered the nightmare of repressed memory therapy gone wrong.

Eventually, this trusted therapist convinced them Steve had multiple personalities

7

and was a part of an underground movement of sodomizers and this is when the police were contacted. His family pressed charges and Steve was arrested.

Steve fought to clear his name, broken and distraught; he determined to expose the truth. The accusations against Steve have been thoroughly investigated and thrown out of court, but the impact it left on his life was traumatic. How could something so bizarre happen to your average American family?

Steve Skotko has become an advocate for victims everywhere and wants to get to the bottom of this and expose the madness. In his own words he shares the nightmare, in which he and his family went through at the hands of an unscrupulous madman. From heartache, to flinging swords, to Nazi Germany - this book has a sci-fi flair to it, yet it is true beyond belief and unfortunately the nightmare still continues.

A book you'll find so dramatic you will have to re-read the evidence over and over before you realize this is big and it isn't a conspiracy theory.

I have to warn you this book is not for the faint of heart.

- Teila Tankersley

<u>ACKNOWLEDGEMENTS</u>

I want to thank everyone in my life who has helped me through all of this including My mother and friend Dorothy Skotko for just being mom.

I also want to thank my best friend in the world Gale Millard for his encouragement, listening ear, and the unending time he spent helping me edit the book.

My co-author Teila Tankersley, she is the best!

I also want to thank the following for their help along the way; Mark, Liz, John S, Rusty, Uncle John, Jan, Cynthia, my Cousin Janice and John L.

A special thank you to my sisters Annelise and Mary Frances for their support, also Frank and Michele Sinclair for the special friendship I have with them and for their spiritual guidance.

I want to extend a special thank you to Staff at my university, which are Brynn, Eric, Anya, Alisha, Ed, and all my instructors.

A special thanks to my attorney Dan, his firm, and his personal staff; Mary and Shelley.

I want to thank everyone at Hillsongs music for producing anointed music. Without it I do not think I would have made it through.

<u>I dedicate this book to my children:</u>

I love you with my whole heart. I pray for the three of you every day. I will always love you and give my life for you. I never hurt you in the ways I have been accused. No matter what anybody says or does, I love you. I have done all I can do to prove I never perpetrated what I was accused of. We are still a family and always will be. Everything being said now is all words of people who carry no credibility or credentials and were not an influence in our family before our involvement with Marion Knox. Don't ever be afraid to call me or contact me. My arms are wide open to you. I hold no bitterness or anything negative against you or anybody else.

If you feel you have suffered abuse in any fashion please contact your local authorities or call your local help line.

Please feel free to contact us at the following email address: helpforvictims@yahoo.com. We are here to help and offer you support.

Forward

Pamela Freyd, PhD
Co-Founder and Executive Director,
False Memory Syndrome Foundation

If ever there was a case, which pointed to the need for better regulation of "therapists," it is the case of Steve Skotko. He was arrested and his family torn apart based on claims of abuse elicited through risky regressive memory therapy.

Regression therapy is risky because of the very real danger of therapeutically induced false "memories." Fortunately for Skotko the Investigation found no evidence for the abuse claims and after two years the case was dropped, but not before creating havoc in Skotko's life.

Skotkos case is not an isolated example, however. Such false accusations have been rampant for the past two decades. Rather than sweep his problems "under the rug," Skotko has confidently decided to tell his story in an effort to warn others of the dangers, which can come from therapists who are not properly trained or monitored. – Pamela Freyd, PhD

Chapter One
Life as I knew it

"Psalm 34:12-13 (NIV). Whoever of you loves life and desires to see many good days, keep your tongue from evil and your lips from speaking lies"

I was sitting in the hallway of the Oregon Health Sciences University on a bright August afternoon waiting for word from the doctor on my wife's condition. She was in surgery now for over two hours for what should have been an easy thirty-minute outpatient surgery. The waiting was just a small part of my experience to date with medical issues concerning my wife. In May of 2008 doctors brought my wife a diagnosis of Hyper-Parathyroidism.[1]

After the discovery of Hyperparathyroidism in May of 2008, local doctors in Albany, Oregon wanted to perform surgery as they had originally discovered the condition. Upon questioning of the doctor in Albany, his surgical procedure was in contrary to specialists we had contacted via the internet.

Dr James Norman who has the website, www.parathyroid.com is a leading specialist in the removal and treatment of Parathyroidism. His website provided a thorough video of the surgical procedure in its entirety and a warning what to look for in a surgeons wrong approach. It was his described "wrong approach," which the surgeons in Albany, Oregon wanted to perform.

Our insurance would not cover the surgery if it were to be performed by Dr. James Norman whose clinic was located in Florida. Faced with her ever increasing symptoms and severe mood swings; I made phone calls to OHSU and was put in touch with the surgeons who would be performing the surgery. I spoke to the doctor directly and questioned the approach they would take. He asked if we could come to Portland the next day to meet with them and have them properly examine and diagnose my wife. This in itself was a miracle.

During this time I was heavily bombarded with verbal assaults from Marion Knox against my character. Knox's assaults would eventually lead to my oncoming nightmare. Looking back over this time, it is easy to see I was on a one-way track to devastation including the loss of many friends along. The individuals could not and cannot to this day understand why I did not see the runaway train speedily approaching me. I felt as If I was sitting in the quiet union station of life merely awaiting a bus when in reality a locomotive was about to run over it.

It is easy to look back and do the "could of, would of, and should have," as the old saying states, along with "hind sight is 20/20" and in my story it was. However, one cannot look back with today's glasses and expect to repair problems viewed with yesterday's spectacles.

In my case the spectacles were the seeds of mistrust, confusion, and suspicion by my family. Miraculously, OHSU telephoned me within a week after the examination and stated they would be able to examine my wife pre-op and schedule her for her surgery in August. I was sitting there thinking of all the doctor's visits, the mood swings, and plethora of accusations and assaults from my soon to be nemesis, Mr. Marion Knox.

Knox had told me on numerous occasions I was the reason for all of my wife's medical issues. He told me, in his opinion; his diagnosis of me was I had in reality, Multiple Personality Disorder. I had a dual personality or multiple personalities in my life. This was how Knox stated it, "you are killing your wife, you are causing the problems with your children, and your daughter's lifestyle is being caused because of your MPD". He reiterated this to me on several occasions. He told my wife the same things on several occasions. Every time we would discover medically the cause for my wife's ailments, he would tell her I had multiple personalities and it in reality was causing her ailments.

Simply put, I refused to receive his counsel and guidance and tried to thwart it away from my wife and children. After my initial visit in 2003, I only went back to his home to try and protect my wife and children. It was only a few visits over the years for me. In every visit Knox emphatically told me to my face and in front of family I indeed had MPD and this was in reality, killing my family and causing my wife's ailments. Knox was adamant in his reasoning.

Knox really believed my supposed psychological problems was somehow creating my wife's physical conditions, and killing her. Knox told me once when I called him on the telephone to confront him and tell him to stop seeing my family; "I am your only hope. I alone can help you, because your problems are spiritual and doctors will not be able to help you".

I was extremely offended at his comments and told him to stay away from my family, and also not see my children any longer. I also told him he was crazy and a "nutcase". He obviously was offended and simply must not have been able to handle my rebuttal and began to attack me verbally in front of my family and behind my back. He convinced my wife and children I was the sole reason behind all their problems.

I would later find out Marion Knox had stated this theory and this train of thought about MPD and other mental disorders in an interview. This interview is posted on the Internet and referred to by Teila Tankersley in chapter twelve.

Marion and Doris Knox adamantly dismissed the ever-increasing amount of open doors and miracles we were receiving from the doctors and the medical community. The Knox's constantly continued to stick to their beliefs and hysteria. All the while my poor wife was caught in the middle of the suggestions and religious mayhem. The Knox's were bombarding her mind, and I believe took advantage of her weakened physical and emotional condition. My wife became even more confused because of the anxiety from her weakened condition due to her very real and medically proven disease.

I grew up a semi-religious person; being raised in a good old-fashioned mid-west catholic home, attending catholic grade and high school. I lived in the same house for the first 18 years of my life. Now, I will be the first to tell you this experience with Knox was way out there In fact this experience was not even in the field of play for me.

I was raised in a lower middle class home of parents who loved each other and unlike the majority of my friends; I had parents who never divorced. I left home at the ripe all knowing age of 18, joined the Air Force and was off to see the world. I met my wife at church just prior to my separation from the military in the summer of 1983. It was in this church and during my time in the United States Air Force, in which I became a born-again Christian.

I will never forget the day I fell in love with her as she sat there on the floor of this historic church building in downtown Colorado Springs. Recently divorced herself with an eight year old son, she sat there praying and crying. At this moment I knew she was a good woman and six months later we began our 25 year marriage to one another. The first awesome responsibility I readily pursued was to raise an eight-year-old stepson on a meager salary as a house painter, my new profession after leaving the Air Force. Now, after twenty-five years it all came down to the knowledge "I supposedly had multiple personalities."

There was so much to take in and so much to digest. There were countless accusations and assumptions. I was now faced with the constant threat of my beloved wife leaving me and taking the children away. I was watching my wife being swept away before my very eyes by a crazy man with all sorts of weird and whacked out ideas and beliefs. I was feeling completely helpless to stop the insanity.

Thinking back now it is all like a crazy dream you cannot wake up from. A nightmare of hellish ideas and accusations; at the same time trying to maintain and run my construction business, which was finally beginning to experience a bit of prosperity. We did not live real well, but on the other hand we did not live badly either. I was able to provide a very nice home for my family. My family was not in want for anything.

I had just completed a nice new addition of a master bedroom to my house. This I did for my wife. Vaulted ceilings, open walls, and plenty of vented skylights gave her a room where she could be comfortable. For years the dark dreary Oregon winters had caused her much depression. Looking back now, through those afore mentioned modern glasses, it was all a result of her Hyperparathyroidism [1] causing a vitamin D deficiency. In preparing the new room for her, I wanted to give her a place where she could have as much natural light as possible. I had already vaulted the ceilings in the kitchen and dining rooms complete with a set of skylights of their own, all for her.

I walked the hallway of OHSU and peered out of the window into the beautiful late summer afternoon in Portland, Oregon. Life outside the hospital hallway looked pretty much average. The newly added tram brought patients from remote parking high up in the air from the additional parking, which was located across Interstate 5. All this light helped me think of all the work I had done in my home to make her life as comfortable as possible.

Yet with all this light, I still felt this overwhelming darkness over my life, as if something was getting ready to transpire. It was an ever-looming dark cloud casting a constant shadow over my life. This whole positive experience with OHSU concerning her surgery was fueled by the previously mentioned trial of mistrust and suspicion instigated by Mr. Marion Knox. The medical help was all opening up to us as quickly as the accusations were coming against me from Knox.

I had first met Mr. Knox in 2001-2002 at the recommendation of a friend. At first, Marion and Doris Knox appeared to be a nice older Christian couple with a desire to befriend and help people. We were struggling a bit with life. We were living in a new house in a new location having moved from Colorado. We had few friends, which were couples. We were looking for some family counseling and friendship to help us a little.

There is no doubt Marion and Doris Knox believe they are genuinely right in their approach I would soon ascertain they were extremely narrow minded and very conceited. After a very short while I found myself not wanting to see or speak to them any longer. However, I would come to realize they continued to relentlessly pursue my wife and eventually my children for their "therapy."

I then heard the doctor call my name, "Mr. Skotko"

Yes, I replied,

"Hello, I am Doctor _____ and the surgery went well. I am concerned though as the tumor on your wife's gland was far larger than we had previously diagnosed."

Is this a problem, I asked?

"No," he said, "It's just your wife's condition is worse than we thought and her recovery will take a bit longer at home."

"How so," I asked.

"Well Mr. Skotko the Parathyroid gland is usually the size of a grain of rice and the gland we removed was approximately the size of a soaked pinto bean, which is by far, bigger than we like for them to get before we recommend surgery. However, she is doing well and you can see her now."

I entered her room; tears filled her eyes. "You stayed?"

"Of course I stayed," I replied, "why would you say such a thing?"

"Well I thought you would have left me and gone home or something."

"Why would I leave you? Sweetheart, I love you!"

I was deeply troubled by these comments.

My wife then looked up at the nurse, held my hand with both of hers and exclaimed, "This is my husband Steve, and he stayed with me after all." The nurse smiled at me and turned away to begin attending to others in the recovery room.

At this moment my mind began to race to a time just a month prior in our lives. My wife and I had been sitting in our car in the parking lot of the Safeway store in Albany, Oregon. She was an emotional mess, which later we would find out was an extreme deficiency of her vitamin D levels. She sat there telling me how I was killing her. My heart felt as if someone was ripping it out of my chest as she said those words.

"Your killing me, I can't take it anymore. I can't cope with it anymore!"

"Cope with what, I asked?"

"Your personalities, Marion told me in reality, you have multiple personalities," she sobbed. (Later I came to find out this was a common accusation, which he would tell most of his victims in the same situation and scenario. "The father figure who was to blame for his families'

25

problems, but refused to believe his therapy")
"Your evil side is killing me," she wailed.

This had been going on now for over nine months; Marion Knox telling her I had multiple personalities. Every medical issue, which arose in her life over the past 9 months we were able to explain, and find the answers for them medically. But, Knox kept badgering her with his insidious mentality; "Her medical issues were a result of my 'multiple personalities.'"

I remember sitting there in the parking lot, wanting to call this Knox guy, and give him a piece of my mind. He was totally brainwashing my wife and I felt as if I could do nothing about it. Often times I would be reminded by my wife how easy it would be for her to leave me and take the children. She stated to me she could easily disappear and this possibility frightened me immensely.

"What do you mean my evil side?" I asked my wife.

"You go in and out of your personalities, even I don't know when you are in which one," she exclaimed.

"All I know is I want it to stop, I hate being this way, and I hate feeling this way."

It would be the next day when we would

get the call about the diagnosis and surgery she would eventually have for her Parathyroid tumor.

We then returned home from the discussion in the parking lot of the store. When we returned home she disappeared for about an hour, after which she came from the bedroom, threw her arms around my neck, hugged and kissed me, and told me how much she loved and appreciated me. I removed her arms from around my neck and asked her, what happened to you? I was completely floored by her comments, what she had just said, and her change of mentality. She had just did a 180 degree flip-flop in her personality right before my eyes.

"Well," she said, "When we got home I went and took a pill I had."

"What kind of a pill and where did you get it?" I asked.

"The doctor gave me a prescription in June because my Vitamin D level was 5?" (This is really low). The Vitamin D pills prescribed were 50,000 IU's and were to be taken once a week. "I feel better," she exclaimed!

I was totally at a loss, I had no idea her Vitamin D was this low, let alone she had seen a doctor for it. One of many things I was to find out was kept from me at the advice of Mr. Knox. I also wondered who really had the multiple personalities going on! He had instructed her not to tell me about the vitamin D issues because as I later found out He told her if I knew, this would take the pressure off of me, and I wouldn't try so hard to retrieve my lost memories of having abused my family.

I found out on many occasions Knox dismissed the doctor's diagnosis and convinced my wife all these problems had a root core, and the root core was I had multiple personalities. Knox also told her "I had sexually molested my children at an early age." I am convinced today he preyed upon her in her weakened state to bring validity to his beliefs.

Later in the evening after the episode at the supermarket parking lot and the vitamin D pill scenario, and prior to the phone call the next morning from OHSU, my wife was lying there in bed. She said she felt awful about what she had said about me and kept apologizing for everything.

The next moment I will never forget, it still puzzles me to this day. As she lay there apologizing to me and looking up at me with tears in her eyes and running down her cheek she asked me this question.
"What do you think of all of this stuff? What do you think of Marion and what he teaches?"

I replied, "I think he is a total nut job, a lunatic, I don't want you talking to him anymore. I want you to get better and heal and I want to find you the right medical doctor who can help you. I think Knox is playing on your emotions, for what reason I don't know, but he is. I would like you to stop talking to him."

At this point I thought she had only occasionally been conversing with him on the telephone. I was actually was quite surprised as to our little altercation in the parking lot of the super market when she had brought up a few of Marion's unusual concepts. It was at this moment, which I feared the greatest for my wife, our marriage and our home.

Her reply to my answer to her question was "This is what I thought you would say," and then she rolled over and completely lost control of her emotions. She would not let me comfort her, touch her or console her in anyway. I had the overwhelming feeling at this time in, which I had completely lost her forever. These episodes of circumstances were a common day in my life during this time.

All of these thoughts came back to me as I sat there and she held my hand in the recovery room. She was actually letting me touch her and console her. She was genuinely shocked I was being kind to her.

After her surgery she could not return to work immediately, so she would spend a lot of time with me in the upcoming month as I was running my business. Being the boss had its advantages and I was basically running from job to job, checking on the crew, and pulling the trailer to the land fill with work refuse. During this time she would just ride with me in the truck. We were able to talk and she seemed as if she was recovering rather well from the surgery at OHSU. She would sit right next to me in the middle of the seat. I felt as if we were twenty years old again and dating. It was so much fun and so intimate to spend these special times with her.

My mind came back to the present as the doctor came by and I asked him,
"How are her Vitamin D levels?"

The doctor told me they were alarmingly low and had already had the nurse give her a pill when she awoke. The doctor stood there and smiled and said, "Mrs. Skotko the surgery was a success, but you are going to feel the effects of the tumor removal for some time. It is going to take about 6-9 months for your hormone levels to level out and for your system to come back into proper balance.

The tumor was larger than we thought and you have probably been feeling the effects of this for quite some time. I determined the tumor to be about 11-12 years old. So please," he asked her, "don't make any life changing decisions for at least 1 yr. Do not change any life insurance or make any rash decisions, which might affect you for at least this long! OK?"

She responded, OK. Before he left the room he stood there and just spent some time talking to her and encouraging her.

We soon left the hospital and returned home. The next month seemed to be so good. We were able to spend a lot of time together. She often accompanied me to work as I said earlier during the day and just rode with me until our youngest son would get home from school. Then it was off to soccer practice or basketball or something.

During the next month, we would drive to the coast every weekend to get away. With our newly acquired chocolate lab, which was now 9 months old, we would have a great time walking on the sand, holding hands, and just spending time with one another. I truly believed she was recovering. Gone were the accusations, the thoughts of my "multiple disorders" and gone I thought were the words and counsel of Mr. Marion Knox.

One month later she would make some decisions, which would thrust me into the worst nightmare of my life, a living hell for the first year; a journey, which is still unfolding. The next two and half years would take me to the deepest depths of despair I would ever go. At times, I would lie in bed, just praying to die. Also during this time I would rediscover myself.

My beliefs in God would be reconstructed. In my greatest despair, I would experience my greatest victories and comfort from God. My complete value system would change. I began to understand people in a new way. My outlook on life would be greatly reshaped and I came to understand my calling in life. Part of this calling is to hopefully never see or let anyone ever experience what I experienced at the hands of people like Marion Knox. I am doing all I can do to stop this man and others from destroying people's lives and causing them shipwreck as a result of unscrupulous therapy.

Notes: Chapter One.

[1] Hyperparathyroidism is the over activity of the Parathyroid gland resulting in excess production of parathyroid hormone (PTH). The Parathyroid gland is not to be mistaken with the Thyroid gland. They are two separate glands in the human body.

The Parathyroid gland produces the Parathyroid hormone PTH. The Parathyroid gland regulates calcium and phosphate levels and helps to maintain these levels. Excessive PTH secretion may be due to problems in the glands themselves, in which case it is referred to as primary Hyperparathyroidism, which leads to hypocalcaemia (raised calcium levels). It may also occur in response to low calcium levels, as encountered in various situations such as vitamin D deficiency or chronic kidney disease; this is referred to as secondary Hyperparathyroidism.

My wife's initial diagnosis was secondary hyperthyroidism. She was suffering with a serious deficiency in Vitamin D levels. Upon further thought later, I concluded it was this condition causing her most of the ailments she was suffering from. This had gone on for years without our knowledge. In all cases, the raised PTH levels are harmful to bone, and treatment is often needed and in most cases mandatory. Recent evidence suggests Vitamin D deficiency/insufficiency plays a role in the development of Hyper-Parathyroidism.

Thus, most of the symptoms of parathyroid disease are "neurological" in origin. Most of the time, it is overlooked for prolonged periods. It is more common than a lot of women think, and the symptoms are merely discarded as Pre-Menstrual Syndrome or Pre-Menstrual Dysphonic Disorder, commonly known as PMS and PMDD.

These were some of the comments the doctors had made to me over time to explain just exactly how this can affect women. Common manifestations of Hyper-Parathyroidism include

- Weakness and fatigue.
- Depression, bone pain, and muscle soreness (myalgias).
- Decreased appetite, feelings of nausea, vomiting and constipation.
- Polyuria (excessive or abnormally large production and/or passage of urine).
- Polydipsia (excessive thirst).
- Cognitive impairment, kidney stones and osteoporosis.

"Mild cognitive impairment (MCI, also known as incipient dementia, or isolated memory impairment) is a diagnosis given to individuals who have cognitive impairments beyond what is expected for their age and education, but do not interfere significantly with their daily activities. It is considered to be the boundary or transitional stage between normal aging and dementia. Although MCI can be present with a variety of symptoms, when memory loss is the predominant symptom it is termed "Amnesia MCI" and is frequently seen as a risk factor for Alzheimer's disease."

Surgical removal of a parathyroid tumor growing on the parathyroid gland will eliminate the symptoms in most patients. The normal size of the Parathyroid gland is a grain of rice. This was the treatment doctors recommended for my wife, the removal of the Parathyroid gland located in the neck. It was a miracle in itself we were even at the OHSU for surgery. Most patients need to have a referral and usually the wait can be very extensive.

(Information concerning Hyperparathyroidism gathered from numerous internet sources and information provided by the Oregon Health Sciences University.)

Chapter Two
The week the walls came crashing down

"Pressure can burst a pipe or pressure can make a diamond." - Robert Horry

"SKOTKO," the intercom screeched.

"Yes", I replied, "get your stuff together and clean up you cell, you made bail." Those words were the best thing I think I heard next to my attorney telling me not to worry because he was getting me out. I made bail, after 3 days I was getting out of jail.

I had never been in jail in my whole life and I do not believe I ever want to go back. What an experience the previous three days had been in a 6 x 12 cell with a 6 inch obscured window to only let in light. Those of you never to of had the opportunity to visit a jail cell, do not worry you are not missing anything. It had been a whirlwind 1-week since the first call from the Albany Police Department. Wednesday September 17, 2008 is a day I will never forget. September 17th is a landmark day in my life as change, and a total redirection of events, which would reshape my life.

My wife and I had spent a long, sleepy, intimate night with each other. On the night before we had been shopping at our local membership club and my wife had me hold her tightly to my side. She was a bit more emotional than she had been for the previous month. Her surgery for Hyperparathyroidism was now in the past. She appeared to be stabilizing and her emotions seemed to be in check.

"I love you so much Steve, I love you so much, she continually told me over and over as we walked the isles; looking for things we needed to buy. My youngest son was off in the toy and video section checking out the available movies; soon to be asking me to buy him a new game for his gaming system.

I asked my wife, "Are you ok?"

"Yes," she replied, "I just love you so much; I just love you so much."

Those words were so good to hear. We had been through so much over the past nine months to a year with everything. I had been wading through a plethora of medical issues, they seemed to never end. We went home this particular evening and just cuddled together and watched re-runs of Stargate SG-1, our favorite relaxing thing to watch during her convalescence.

I was now awake and ready to tackle a new day. It was Thursday and I was up and in the shower when my wife asked me if she could make me breakfast. My favorite, ham and cheese omelet with hash browned potatoes. Things seemed like they would be all right. Then again, this was the way it all seemed for the past nine months, one minute everything was good, then the next there seemed to be total confusion. Daily life was an emotional pendulum; it swung back and forth, now it seemed to be swinging more quickly. Life was back and forth, and at times life's pendulum seemed to swing by the hour.

"What time you think you will be home for lunch," she asked, as we ate breakfast together. "Probably the usual, about 11:30," I replied.

"Do you want to go with me this afternoon, maybe we can get a cup of coffee, and I have a lot of running to do today."

"This sounds good," she replied, "I think I would like this a lot," she stated. Then my son entered the room,

"I missed the bus," he said.

"It's ok" I replied, I'll drive you to school.

My wife interrupted, "No, I'll take him"

For a brief moment we struggled with the decision. She did not want me to drive him to school. As my son and I drove to his school he was a bit on the quiet side,

"I love you dad," he said.

"I love you to son, are you O.k.?"

"Are you going to come to my soccer game this weekend?"

"Of course I will, you know I come to all of your games!"

"I know, but you will be there won't you?"

"Yes of course I will"

"Are you sure you are O.K. son?

"Yeah, I am alright," as he exited the truck.

"I love you son,"

"I love you to dad," he said glumly as he closed the truck door and headed into school.

This was a very strange conversation I had with him. It puzzled me all morning. After I dropped him off I returned home and grabbed my calendar. Then with a swift kiss goodbye to my wife, I was off to the job. Little did I know those were the last words I was to have with my son as well as the last words I would ever speak to my wife. Later I would discover my son had already had a visit from a social worker at school from the DHS without my knowledge and kept from me by my wife. He had already had an interview at the DHS office with Susan Juster, the caseworker.

The next day when I was served with a restraining order it dawned on me; they knew, they all knew. My wife had it planned to turn me over and call the police. I discovered a bit later during the trial in May 2009 she had gone to the DHS to seek advice. She knew for 4 months. My wife had told my children to not say a word. No wonder my son asked those questions. He knew something was going to happen. He knew I would not be at his soccer game. Little does he know I was there, more than 150' away watching him through my binoculars!

I did not have a very eventful day. Normally it would have been, but with everything transpiring, it seemed rather boring this day. I returned home at 11:30 and expected to find my wife home waiting for me, but she was not there. I tried to phone her, but her cell phone was turned off. I grabbed some lunch and waited till about 12:15 and when she did not return or I could not reach her by phone, I left. I drove pulling my dump trailer to the landfill.

I left the pit after dumping the trailer and my cell phone rang, "Hello Mr. Skotko, this is detective Fairall with the Albany police department. We received a report from Peggy Skotko about an alleged report of domestic violence, where could we meet you to discuss this alleged incident?" (Note here he said domestic violence). I was at a complete loss for words as I wondered what in the world they were talking about. I met with the detective and his partner at the local truck stop. When I got there they were waiting for me.

"Mr. Skotko," he asked.

"Yes this is me", I replied.

"Mr. Skotko I lied to you, your wife called us and reported you of sexually molesting your

41

children." (Note here, the police admitted lying. I really discovered later the police lie a lot!)

I still hear those words in my mind. It was as if something cut me in half. I was numb. I felt as if someone just cold cocked me with a 2X4. I was stunned, my head began to swim, my heart felt as if a huge spear had been thrust through it. I wobbled where I stood. I staggered to my trailer to sit down on the workbox attached to the front of it. Both detectives reached for their guns to draw them at me.

I said, "No No, I just need to sit down, I think I am going to pass out."

"Mr. Skotko I lied to you, we are going to have to have you follow us down to the police station for questioning."

"Very well, I will."

"Just follow us and please don't try to flee."

I got back into my truck and followed them to the police station. As I followed them I reached to phone my attorney, there was no answer but I left a message on his cell phone. I don't know what moved me to phone my attorney, I just did. I arrived at the police station still confused as to what the heck was happening to me. I was in a stasis of tunnel vision. It was as if the whole world was closed to me. I didn't think. I just functioned! I followed the detective into the station and he led me to an interrogation room.

It was exactly like you would see on a classic television show. There was one table, two chairs and the room was fashioned with a one-way window with the mirror on my side.

"Would you like to have something to drink," he asked.

"Yes, I'd like a glass of water."

"You might as well turn off your phone," He stated, "this room is shielded, and so you can't receive any calls in here." He left the room, (another lie.)

As soon as he left the room, I looked at my cell phone and there was no signal. This is great, I thought, I couldn't even talk to Dan. I really liked my attorney; he had already helped me out a lot. Not more than 10 seconds later, as I held the phone in my hand, still flipped open, my cell phone rang and it was my attorney.

"Steve, do not say a word, not a single word to them. You tell them you want your attorney present. They will get mad, but they will let you go. When they do, get your ass down here to my office and we will talk, bring all your financial stuff, all your credit cards, and your check book."

Dan was right and it happened just as he said, they let me go. As I was leaving detective Fairall started mocking me in the following way, "Hey Steve what about what Marion told us," he bellowed at me across the parking lot, "What about it," He yelled.

"You better not say anything to your wife or son if you see them, if you do, I will hunt you down myself and kick the shit out of you," He yelled. Then he just started screaming at me, "Do you understand me, I will come and kick your ass!" This was the glorious law enforcement professional we had working in Albany, Oregon. "My gosh," what was happening, It seemed the whole world was flipping out all around me.

I just shook my head and got into my truck and went home. I got to my home, unhooked my trailer, grabbed all the things Dan told me to bring and left for his office. As I was leaving, a social worker with the Department of Child Services came by with a deputy sheriff.

"Mr. Skotko I need to speak with you." "I am sorry but I have been directed by my attorney to speak with nobody until I speak with him." I replied.
I got into my truck and began to leave. This woman by the name of Susan Juster got irate and began shouting at me as I drove off. "I will make

your life a living hell!" From this moment she made it her goal to make my life a living hell. I drove off and went to Dan's office.

Dan asked me "what in the hell is going on Steve."

"I don't know Dan", and then I told him what had been transpiring and about where I thought all this was coming from, Mr. Marion Knox.

"Well Steve this is what I want you to do. Go to the bank, take as much money as you can off your credit cards, joint bank accounts and open another account in your name only and deposit all the money in it.

"She has declared war on you. You are going to need it for bail. They will arrest you soon and you are going to need it." He went on to tell me; "You are going to have to get tough, suck in all your emotions. Call me no matter what time it is." I left with his assurances. "Call me tomorrow and then on Saturday, stay in touch I am here to help you."

Dan has been a fantastic confidant to me for the past 3 years. His legal savvy and advice saved me from a lot more pain and eventually from a long prison sentence from something I did not do. I did as he said and opened the account the next morning, which was Friday.

Thursday night was the loneliest, darkest, scariest night of my life. So many emotions ran through my head. I was numb. The pain was too great for me to bear. I truly believe God himself came into my bedroom and stood by my side, or at least He sent an angel to watch over me.

The hurt was so deep; I could not believe this was happening to me. My kids, my kids I kept telling myself. I woke up every half hour, one time in a sweat, the next freezing cold. My emotions were off the chart. I just lay there crying, hurting, wailing, angry, sad, and then hurt all over again.

It is so difficult to put into words the betrayal I felt, and the longing for my son and two oldest children. I just kept thinking of them, and I still do every day since. I laid there for a while and then all the emotions would come flooding back into my heart, mind and soul. I felt so violated. It was as if my adversary was standing right there beating the crap out of me. My adversary was kicking me, biting me, punching me as if it had the free will to do so.

I got up the next morning and opened up the new bank account. Surprisingly enough, I went to work the next day and finished up a few things and then returned home. I was exhausted, mentally drained, and completely worn out.

As I prepared to lie down and take a nap, my pup just came over to me and sat beside me and just put its head on my lap and snuggled his snoot right up in my lap. It was as if the dog knew I was hurting. I was hurting bad, real bad. I wanted to throw up; a few times I had the dry heaves.

The pain was so great in my chest; I cannot describe how I felt. As I lay down to take a nap, I heard a knock at the door. I went to the front door and there was a Linn County Sherriff officer at my door.

"Mr. Skotko," "Yes" I replied.

"I have to serve you this restraining order. You have 20 minutes to get all of your stuff and get off of these premises." "You are kidding?" I replied.

"No sir I am not, you will also have to refrain yourself from within 150 feet of the property."

It was all happening so quickly, I could not even think. I could not believe this was happening to me. It took everything I possessed to get a suitcase and throw my clothes and a few personal items in it. I gathered what I could and left. I was running all over the house trying to think of what to grab. They would not even let me take anything regarding my business or tools or anything.

I had to be gone. Little did I know this would be the last time I would ever see the inside of my house, my shop, and my youngest son from this day forward. I would never see any of my tools, business assets, computers or anything else from my life ever again. All the possessions we had gathered and shared together for nearly 25 years were gone. Family pictures, my books, CD's, Videos, It was and is all gone.

Poof! My life as I knew it ended right there, right then. Everything I knew is gone. I want to ask you the readers of this book; stop right now and look around you. Examine your life, close your eyes and reflect on your life. Take a moment and think about all you have. Look at your home, the furnishings in it, your children, and your vehicles. Stop and inventory your life, think about all the things you take for granted. Things and stuff in your life, which are there but you take for granted.

All pictures of the baby, pictures of your kids growing up, pictures of their birthday parties you have placed in a box and put on a shelf in the closet or storage. Now imagine all of it and more, in a split second, it's all gone. Better yet, it's still all there, but you can't touch it, you can't have it anymore. In this sense, it's all gone! Let this thought soak into your heart! This is what happened to me, I lost everything!

The upcoming weekend starting on Friday night I stayed at a hotel in Albany, Oregon; trying to regroup and figure out what the heck was going on. I had received a telephone call from my mother. It was the first time I had spoken with her in over five years.

My relationship with family in Ohio had become strained over the previous five years, most of it due to the fact my wife did not trust them. Marion Knox had persuaded my wife my parents, being Catholic, had subjected my children to abuse and other forms of ritual abuse.

I cannot begin to explain how during the same five years, my mind and emotions had been squeezed into such a small box even to have gone along with this madness. Being so busy with my business, dealing with my wife's medical issues, raising the children, football games, basketball games, and hearing the barrage of threats from my wife she was going to leave me and take the children. On a number of occasions I would witness my wife sitting in the dark garage for hours on end speaking on the phone with Marion Knox and others. The threats of my wife calling the police to turn in my mother for allegedly abusing the children had me reeling at times.

Phone calls came from Mr. Knox trying to persuade me he could help me. I caved in to the pressure. I let myself get estranged from my family. I wrote letters, which were false to them, bringing accusations, which were not true. I can truly say with all honesty a day did not go by when I did not think of my family in Ohio. I wanted to telephone them, I wanted to reconcile with them, but I had no idea where to begin.

I regret the decision to stop communication with my family in Ohio. I was wrong to believe those accusations. I was wrong to let my emotions and feelings get entangled. I hurt my mother. I regret all those decisions I had made during this time when it came to my family. Today my relationship with my mother has been restored. My relationship with the rest of my family is still a work in progress.

I have learned to enjoy eating Crow! Fried, diced, sautéed, breaded, Barbequed, you name it and I have eaten crow. I talked with my mother on this Friday evening for 2 hrs. I felt so horrible. When they heard the accusations, they rallied to my defense. They have all been such an encouragement to me. I have three wonderful nephews and a new brother-in-law whom I am getting to know. It is all a work in progress. I love all of them with my whole heart.

50

This whole story of my reuniting with my family in Ohio is a miracle in itself. It was my family in Ohio who sent the extra needed funds to be bailed out of jail. To lend even more to this story, my mother informed me when I phoned her and left a message, this day was the last day she would have the same telephone number. The next day Saturday, she was moving and would have a new number. Had I not contacted her this day, she would have been out of touch and I would not have been able to contact her. No one would have known her telephone number. Three days later I was arrested. Without my mother I would have had spent a lot longer in jail. This is just one testimony I have of miracles happening in my life through this ordeal.

Everyday has produced circumstances, which have worked in my behalf. I refer to them as miracles, because I believe they are. They are nothing short in my mind they are miracles. In the midst of all those miracles there was brewing even more betrayal, more deceit, more lying than I could have ever imagined. These issues would fester in my life like one huge zit! It was big and ugly, like a huge beast snarling, waiting to pounce on me, and attempting to devour me whole. It is an ugly vile vermin, waiting to sink its teeth into me. It did and it would change my life forever.

A few days later I would be arrested and jailed for 3 days. During those three days I would sink to my lowest depths. During those same three days I would have the most exhilarating experience. It changed my life forever. My thought processes would change. The way I viewed people would change. My emotions were all over the page. What was happening to me? It was as if I would wake up at times and wonder what reality was, and what the nightmare was.

Chessboard by Anna Cervova

Chapter Three
Establishing a Team to weed through the lies

"A successful man is only as good as the people he surrounds himself with." Ronald Reagan

Stepping aside from my story, I want to say, "I believe you can never have too much input or gather to much information. The more you have the better chance you have at finding the adequate solutions and implementing the necessary plan to solve issues present in your life. Team concept and team participation are exactly this, 'TEAMS.' At some point all on the team may contribute equally, at times certain individuals will have more idea's based on their own unique set of circumstances, work history and experience. Also, at times you will have no answers and see no way out of your circumstances. It is at those times you have to trust completely in your team.

I believe the hardest part of Teams is being willing to step aside when another member has the insight or ideas we may not have. What comes around goes around. A wise individual will realizes he/she will not always have the best solution at any given time, and will surround themselves with people they feel will step forward at any given time and assess the situation. They permit individuals on the team to assess the situation as needed without letting their ego's or pride get involved in determining what is needed to solve the problem at hand."

My friends this really sums up a lot of things, which have transpired in my life. I realized very quickly this whole process, which was beginning to unfold in my life would take a team approach. We would need the families who have been affected prior to me to step forward and speak out yet again to the insidious practices of Marion Knox and others like him.

I am able now to make sense of some things, but only after two and half years of soul and heart searching. I knew my life would be forever changed. Initially I may not have wanted this to happen. In my mind I wanted things to return to what they were. I am so very happy for others who have had their lives turned upside down by Marion Knox and his barbaric therapy, experiencing a healing and restoration of their families and homes.

The wave of opposition is overwhelming due to the fact this man is well known throughout the west coast for his gospel music and singing. It took me awhile to accept some things, but I began to realize people were exiting my life because of this, and this hurt. Some things to this day I still struggle to accept and believe. I know now and believe with my whole heart my wife and children was never my enemy. They were and are victims just like I had been. It seemed as if betrayal was a daily event in my life. Like I stated, it has been two and one half years now, and I am continually discovering and realizing how things were and how they became what they became.

I want to go on record to everyone who may hear my voice or read these words; I never have or will I ever claim I was perfect.

There were so many false accusations brought against me. I regret others were led to believe those accusations as the truth and acted upon them. I have no problems owning up to my mistakes and making amends for them. I unconditionally love my children. I love them with my whole heart. To this day I would give my life for them. I believe in my heart the Albany Police Department and the arresting detective made huge mistakes in how they handled this situation. I wish I could bring them into accountability for their great blunder. The following is a clip from the Albany Democrat herald dated October 14, 2002. It gives amazing facts into my story of another man who went through what I went through with great similarity.

"DA's office drops charges against Brownsville man.

Story; By Les Gehrett:
Albany Democrat-Herald | Posted: Monday, October 14, 2002 12:00 am

` The Linn County District Attorney's Office has dropped all charges it filed a year ago against a Brownsville man, and the case against him has been closed.

Senior Deputy District Attorney George Eder confirmed the case against Roger David McCracken, 36, was closed and would not be reopened.

"Our office examined the evidence in preparation for trial and came to the conclusion there was insufficient evidence to support a conviction," Eder said.

The case was scheduled to go to trial in late September, but the DA's office filed a motion to dismiss the charges on Sept. 5, and the order was made final on Sept. 9.

McCracken was charged on Oct. 30, 2001, with several sex-related crimes. All of the charges related to a single alleged incident with a minor girl. This incident was alleged to have occurred in late September of the same year. Court records showed McCracken's defense team had uncovered evidence-casting doubt on whether the alleged incident ever occurred.

A motion filed in June 2002 by attorney Stephen R. Ensor of Corvallis summarized the defense's case.

Ensor wrote at some point early last fall, before any allegations against McCracken were made, the alleged victim was taken by her mother to Good Samaritan Hospital for an emergency psychological evaluation.

"It was reported to the emergency room staff the child had been seen by a faith-based counselor who was versed in 'casting out demons.' It is also noted the family is extremely religious. There was concern about the alleged victim's episodes of violent behavior and periods where she was completely unresponsive, as if unconscious." Hospital staff recommended further consultation should be performed with the child's pediatrician and a full psychiatric work-up completed, according to the defense motion.

"It is unknown whether a psychiatric work-up was initiated, but it does appear the child was taken to Marion Knox, who we believe to be the faith-based counselor referred to in the emergency room records. The family had known Marion Knox for an undetermined period of time," Ensor stated.

The defense team contacted a number of people who are acquainted with Marion Knox. Three of these people made statements to investigators and said they were willing to testify "concerning Mr. Knox's preoccupation with and belief many people he has counseled with, have been sodomized," Ensor stated.

"It is believed the sodomy allegation against Mr. McCracken was made following counseling with Marion Knox," Ensor wrote.

"In the three cases cited by the defense, Knox had concluded there had been sodomy even though the families said there had not been, according to the court file."

Contacted by phone this morning, Knox said he had not been contacted by either the defense or the prosecutors in this case. Knox declined further comment.

McCracken also declined to comment about the charges against him being dropped. When he was indicted last November, it was reported McCracken was a trained opera singer who had taught at East Linn Christian Academy.

Like I stated, I have no problem accepting responsibility for my actions. The greatest frustration at this point is the realization my wife and children resent me for things I did not do, yet they believe I did. They harbor resentment based on what Marion Knox has taught them, saying it did happen, when in fact it did not.

My wife and children at first did not believe it, but this man Knox pressed them into believing they did happen. This is a huge pill to swallow and accept. This particular case reported by the local newspaper happened six years prior to mine. In the article it states the defense attorney had witnesses who stated similar incidents prior to this one. This type of counseling by Marion Knox has been going on for a long time. When will it stop? When will the authorities step in and put a stop to it? This is why I knew it would take a team effort to attempt to make the insanity stop. It has been in the works now for over 2 years. It is a work in progress. It is going to stop!

I know, I know, this is what everyone says. Every person who is in jail today or even prison will tell you to your face they are innocent of all charges. I really do not want, nor am I attempting to position myself on the peach basket in an attempt to preach my innocence. There was documented proof in the Albany Police Departments possession, along with a little wise detective work, would have shed a lot of light to this fact. This article would have shed some light onto Marion Knox and what he is all about and how he functions. There could have been a much more responsible decision made on the parts of detective Fairall and his associates, which could have been reached.

Sad to say no matter what I may do, what tests or examinations I may take, nothing will change the minds of those "responsible" parties. Being a man in today's world can have its setbacks. There are a lot of perverted people out there in the world. There are individuals who prey upon innocent children and women. We read and watch on the news, both local and national, about men who target children and women and exploit them.

Within the last year here in Cleveland, Ohio, we saw the atrocities perpetrated by Anthony Sowell. This individual over a period of 10 years raped and murdered young African American women in Cleveland's east side. After doing this he buried them and hid the remains in the back yard or the walls of the house. There was such a stench at times in the neighborhood people called the police. It was discovered most of the explanations for bad odors in the neighborhood were dismissed as coming from a local sausage shop.

Now I will be the first to step up and agree people like this, people who exploit children to pornography and abuse, and those who mistreat animals are all in the same category and need to be dealt with and punished to the fullest extent of the law.

61

2009-2010 brought with it "Jessica's Law" to stop child molesters in their tracks. On the other hand today's society has yielded itself to a modern day witch-hunt. If a man is erroneously accused of touching someone inappropriately, they can be jailed and lose everything overnight. They are stuck in a jail and have to fight to prove their innocence. A person of the opposite sex can simply dislike you and with one phone call have you jailed for something you never even thought of doing.

People get appalled when this is said, yet it is true. There are many men and women who have had to weave themselves through the maze of our justice system to prove their innocence. It cost tens of thousands of dollars and much grief and agony to prove ones innocence.

I have accepted what happened (I do not agree) and I choose to function on the team the Good Lord has placed me on. As I stated in the first paragraph of this chapter, I learned quickly in this scenario; I would need to trust the members on this team. I now understand there were individuals in my life who were beginning to exit and new ones who began to enter it.

I have discovered this is a healthy process and have accepted it. I would learn very quickly to trust the advice of my attorney, other close friends, and new individuals introduced to me. I know without a doubt God removed people from my life who would not function as a team. They were letting preconceived ideas about me cloud their opinion of me concerning this issue. These individuals although good became biased with examining the evidence or lack of it and would have caused further detriment in my life had they stayed.

It became a daily event in my life; individuals I believed were friends betrayed me, and formed opinionated one-sided conclusions. I had a friend for years I would travel with and help, due to physical disabilities. He believed the opposition without even asking me about things. He was a person I shared my heart with and inner most feelings. He never even had any contact with my wife. He just simply chose to believe her without ever contacting me.

This friend I telephoned and left a message with called me back on my home phone, which he never did before and spoke with my wife for the first time in years. On this occasion he called me on the home phone but before he had always called me on my cell phone. He chose to believe her, even though he knew me. Does this make him and all the rest my enemy? I do not believe so, however, it also left me with decisions as to whom I would place around myself and trust in my life.

I began to see the true character of some people in my life. I began a long hard lesson about things about myself I never saw before. I am probably one of the best friends a person can have. I am an extremely loyal person. I never draw conclusions immediately, however when faced with a tremendous amount of data and information have no problem in letting people go and making difficult decisions regarding individuals. One of my favorite scriptures in the bible goes something like this, very paraphrased so all individuals will understand.

"I would rather be the janitor in a mansion with a few friends, than to dwell in the luxurious chambers of the house with a multitude of contentious half-hearted people!" Yes sir, in my own words, *"I would rather clean toilets and have one loyal friend, than to be CEO and have fair weathered friends."*

I learned there was and will be three types of individuals in my life. I learned and am learning who they are, and in what role they function in my life. I love them all dearly, but I learned where to categorize them and maintained the faith to keep them there in this role in my life. They are people of all shapes and sizes, female

64

and male, people of all races and back rounds. They are people of all religious persuasions and back rounds.

I could not and cannot be one-dimensional any longer in my life. It is their character I have learned to watch. It is their character you need to watch. These individuals will enter and leave your life. They will come and go. Not all of them will be friends, some you may despise and detest. Some could be what you call friends. This is why I like to refer to them as individuals.

These are the three types I have learned function in my life, and I believe if you closely examine yours and be honest with yourself, are present in your life as well. There are a multitude of individuals who will come in and out of your life, who will bless you and help you. You cannot limit yourself. You have to live out of the box so to say. I had to stop being narrowed minded and one-dimensional. You must stop being narrow and one-dimensional if you are ever going to heal from being hurt and having suffered abuse. Bishop T.D. Jakes so eloquently described this in a video I watched at a very difficult time in my life.

The "Confidant" – "These are individuals who are for you. They believe in you

65

because they are your friends. No matter what
may happen to you or what decisions you make
in life, they are for you, Period! You will have
very few of them in your life. They love you
unconditionally. They are into you. They love
you when you are up, and they love you when
they are down. They love you when you are
right, and they love you when you are wrong.
They are into you for the long haul. If you get
your hands dirty, they get dirty hands with you. If
you land in the jailhouse, they come and visit
you. The will come to you and commune with
you when you are living in the dump, or when
you are living in the mansion. They are into you!

Your confidant will mentor you. He or
She, will help you get over the walls in your life.
Their love is unconditionally. They are the ones
who feed you. Most of us have people under us
who we feed in life. After a while these under
you will drain you. Your Confidant is on the
same level with you. They will feed you when
you are hungry in life. When you need a good
word, they will bring it to you. They listen to
you. The Confidant is intimately intertwined with
you in your life. They are there to help you reach
your destiny. They will confront you. They will
"get in your face." They will get into your
business. They will tell you when you are wrong

because they are your Confidants. They are into you! You will have very few of them in your life."

Bishop Jakes went on to say; "If you are fortunate enough to have two or three of these types of individual's in your life, then you are a very blessed person. Without them you will never be the person you are called to be. You need to find your Confidant."

We would all hope to have at least one in our life. If we are married for any period of time then we would think, at best, our spouse would be this individual. However, this might not always be the case!

The "Constituents"- "They are not into you, like the Confidant, they are into what you are for. As long as you are for what they are for, they will walk with you. They will labor with you, and they will work with you. Never think they are for you. They are for what you are for. Never forget this, as soon as they meet someone else who will further their agenda, they will leave you and hook up with the other because they were never for you. They are just for what you were for.

Throughout your life if you are not careful, especially when you are broken and struggling, you will mistake your Constituents for your Confidants. You will think they are for you, when in reality they were never for you, they were never into you, and they aren't ever going to be there for you. Just about the time you fall in love with them they will break up with you and hook up with somebody else because they were never for you. It was never about you, but for the causes you represent. They are your Constituents!"

Sad to say a lot of people will never accept this. They will constantly try and make their Constituents into their Confidants. Are you struggling with relationships, over and over again? Maybe you are mistaking your Constituents for your Confidants. Maybe you are sharing you deep dark secrets and feelings with someone who was never into you, only into what you were for because it gave their agenda credibility. I did this for a long time. It was hard to accept the idea those I thought were Confidants were merely Constituents. When they left my life, I was devastated.

The "Comrades"- "These people are not for you, nor are they for what you are for; it is they are against what you are against. The Comrades make for strange bedfellows. This will cause people to come together who are not for you, nor are they for what you are for, but they are against what you are against. This will cause people to team up together with you to help fight a greater enemy. Do not be confused by their association, they will only be with you until the victory is accomplished.

They are like scaffolding; they come into your life for a purpose. When the purpose is complete the scaffolding is removed. Do not be upset when the scaffolding is removed because the building always remains.

Expect the Constituents and the Comrades to leave you and desert you after a while. Do not be upset when they do not react to your dream the way you wanted them to react because they were never really with you in the first place. Be careful who you tell your dreams to, in which you bear your soul to. If you tell your dream to your constituents they will desert you and try to fulfill the dream without you. If you tell your dream to your Comrades they won't support you because they were never with you or for you in the first place. They were only against what you were against. You can tell those who are really for you because they will weep with you when you weep. They will rejoice with you when you rejoice.

They won't interject "advice" or "bring direction into your life" unless you first ask, or unless you have established them as a Confidant.

When you walk into a large room and tell people your good news, stop and watch everyone's reaction to your good news. If they are not happy for you, just shut your mouth and walk back out of the door. Nothing you do or say can make them for you. Stop right there and save yourself a lot of heartache, grief, and rejection.

If people are really connected with you then they will be happy for you when you share your dream. They will be on board with you when you are getting ready to face your struggles. They will be an unending encouragement to you no matter how dark or grave the circumstances you are facing or about to face. When you or a loved one are sick or in the hospital, they are right there to visit you, pray for you and encourage you through your sickness.

When the garbage truck of life dumps on your existence and you are in the middle of a mess, they are the ones who show up with shovels, pickup trucks and perfume to help you clean up your surroundings. One thing I have learned is this; I am truly thankful for the people who have come into my life through my ordeal. I am no longer upset with the people who have chosen to exit my life. Sad to say this is my ex-spouse and my children. They have chosen this based on a lie. I cannot change this. I will not beg people to love me. I will not persistently pursue a relationship with those who have chosen to exit my life.

I will however pray for them. If they are in trouble or facing a crisis, I will be the first one there to help them. If they ever need help I will be right there for them. Outside of the few people who are your Confidants, or the ones who have chosen you as a Confidant, there is only one unconditional love, which is for your children. I love my children unconditionally no matter what may happen. I love my children unconditionally no matter what they may say or chose to believe. I love my children!

The team in your life will be the most important thing you establish. Your team will keep you. You will never be in a darker place than God permits for you. God will always send somebody into your life to help you. You are never alone. When you are led to walk through these dark valleys, God will always provide an escape for you. "If God leads you to it, He will bring you through it."

It was about six months after my journey began, in which I really began to realize the enormity of the situation. I would never be the same and I would start making crucial choices in my life. I began to realize and it was confirmed through my Confidants, this was a mission. I would have to make some hard choices. If I did not make those decisions, others down the road might be as affected as I was. I could have easily buried myself under a bottle of alcohol or other choices of escape. I do not wish to offend anyone who has chosen to follow this course. I was determined I would make a difference to see the suffering of others be less or non-existent.

My life has been enriched with individuals who have been affected in the same manner as me by Marion Knox. I am so proud others are stepping forward and declaring their stories. What is unfolding is a pattern to brain wash people into believing this lie. Knox systematically leads people down a road, which leads to the same outcome, broken lives and families torn apart because of his whacked out hysterical beliefs. One really begins to wonder who is abusing people more in the long run. You the reader must not accept all of this solely on my word alone. We will present hard evidence and personal testimonies of others who have endured this same barbaric therapy and council provided by Knox.

Autumn Fire by Mark Coldren

Chapter Four
Trying to make sense of it all

"Though God slays me, yet will I trust in him: but I will maintain mine own ways before him."
Job 13: 15

This chapter is as the title says, "Trying to make sense of it all." It is an injustice to think I can do this in one chapter of one book. This whole experience and especially this chapter can and will be a whole book in itself. Through this whole nightmare there are a few prevailing

73

questions, which always arise when I try to make sense of it all, and what others seem to ask me as they try to help me make sense of it all. Here are those questions,

-How could something like this happen?

-Isn't there something you could do to stop this man?

-Why have not other's stopped him if it's been going on for 30 years? Can't you bring suit against him or someone else? And the biggest question of them all is this, why does this man do this? And what is his agenda?

I will admit for the most part I believe I have handled this situation fairly well. There are times I got angry. There are moments now I feel angry. There are times I was angry with God, angry with friends, angry with the clerk at the store, angry at the gas stationed attendant and angry with the person driving in front of me!

It was Thanksgiving day, 2008. I remember it was a regularly dreary day. I took myself to a park in Salem, Oregon were others were helping serve Thanksgiving dinner to homeless people. It was a day I determined my anger had to stop. My anger reached its apex. It was a cold day, really cold. It was the day of our 25th wedding anniversary. Suddenly the peace came, the overwhelming, unspeakable peace and

A Heart Held Ransomed

contentment rested upon my heart, soul, and total being. Standing there in the wind and rain, helping others, seeing them all there with no food, no clothing, and no teeth!

There was a special couple I sat next to as I ate my own helping of water soaked Thanksgiving dinner.

"Thank you," she said. "It's so nice to have a nice dinner today." I just sat there and looked at them. They were dirty, smelly, but it was the smile, which went from ear to ear, which finished me off. I did not say a word and I could barely get 20 feet from the pavilion when the flood of tears came.

I think my eyes produced more water this particular afternoon than did the skies. From this moment until this day, the love of God has flooded my heart. The peace and resolve only God can bring entered my soul. I went back to my hotel room and just cried for hours. All I wanted to do was stop this mayhem from ever happening to anyone else ever.

If I were God Almighty, I would know the answers to those questions above in this chapter. However, while I draw breath on this earth I may never know the answers to these questions, nor will I understand them. I will say the most common remark I hear when I share my

75

story is, "Man dude! This has to be the weirdest, most outlandish, strange, odd (and a whole host of other synonyms) story, which I have ever heard." I thought long and hard as to what I would pen for this chapter and I come up with a paper I wrote for an ethics class at the university I would like to put here. I would ask you bear through it and I will give my thought and insight at the end. The subject for the paper I had never heard of or what had happened to this group of people, and it was transpiring in our world and it concluded when I was a child.

I did the research as I was taking the class. I hope it is thought provoking for you as it was for me. Try to place yourselves into either pair of shoes, the one's conducting and the one's being treated (or so they thought). So here we go!

"Every person or family member who has faced a medical crisis during his or her lifetime has at one point hoped for an immediate cure, a process would deter any sort of painful or prolonged convalescence. Medical research always has paralleled a cure or treatment. From the beginning of the turn of the 20th century the most unspeakable appalling atrocities against human beings was The Tuskegee Syphilis Study. One of the most horrendous breaches of ethics in

76

The United States history is Tuskegee's studies and associated research.

The study and the publicity surrounding the study was one of the major influences leading to the organized arrangement of laws, rules and principles of the ethical treatment for human beings. Examples of which include; informed consent, patients personal autonomy, patients' bill of rights, medical code of ethics, and limits to a practitioners professional autonomy.

Miracle cures like penicillin and other antibiotics have proven the value of research. Many illnesses and diseases are currently under heavy research. Although not much research can give results, which penicillin or other antibiotics have attained does not invalidate the necessity of research and the importance of it. There exist copious treatments for diseases today previously diagnosed terminal. Today those treatments extend life, which just a few years ago would have killed or disabled it.

Hope is a powerful weapon in the minds of those facing medical dilemmas. Hope can bring a confidence and trust between a patient and his or her medical specialist. The final and crowning moment of medical research is to convey hope and medical therapy will succeed and alleviate a patient's pain and suffering.

Today's medical community must convey to patients the need for research and development. A working supportive approach with an individual's caregiver will leave a lasting impression on individuals succumbing to the ravages of disease. A patient facing certain death should have the advisement to permit consent for radical and daredevil treatments. Participation is paramount for both sides to produce results.

The effective worth of research has a more sound foundation when maintained in a confined and controlled environment (Foster, 2001).

Medical treatment has advanced immensely from the beginning of the 20th century. Atrocities have plagued human history, which society looks back on as cruel and sadistic. The end of the Second World War brought information and pictures of the appalling treatment of the Jewish people by Hitler's Germany. Paralleled to those treatments in history was the Tuskegee study.

African Americans were the focal point of the Tuskegee study in 1928, the apex of the United States time in history referred to as the roaring twenties. American citizens were enjoying a time of illustrious prosperity and revelry. During this time the Chicago-based charity named the Julius Rosenwald Fund contacted The United States Public Service about ways to enhance and improve the health care African Americans received living in the south, which at this point in history was nonexistent.

During this same time the United States Public Service was just ending a study on the prevalence of Syphilis among black employees of the Mississippi-based Land Company named Delta Pine. As the treatment program began at the same time the great depression struck the United States of America, The Rosenwald Fund withdrew its support being struck very hard by the great depression.

Due to the withdrawal of the Rosenwald Fund and for insurance of success the Public Health Service garnished the support of the Tuskegee Institute because Tuskegee had a positive repor and history of service to the Black community. In return Tuskegee had the security its nurses and interns received training and employment. To garnish support Tuskegee contacted local church leaders, community leaders, and plantation owners. No record exists of garnishment of consent of the participants.

One of the ongoing debates occurring during this time was the possibility of racial variation in the effects of syphilis. A Public

79

Health Service doctor by the name of Taliaferro Clark suggested this syphilis study would not fail by studying the effects of syphilis on untreated living subjects. Taliaferro Clark's suggestion was adopted and a study set in motion.

During this time in American History African Americans had virtually no health coverage to speak of, and most of the participants never had any sort of examination ever. Study participants received medical examinations. Examinations were free along with transportation and food. Benefits of the study were not made known and no therapeutic research conducted would benefit the participants.

Study participants were told nothing of their infection with syphilis. Treatment was withheld from participants, and no satisfactory treatment given for satisfactory recovery to a few. Public Health System officials denied study participants treatment and prevented other medical professionals and agencies from supplying medication and treatment.

Another alarming fact resulting from the study is the United States Draft Board requested 50 of the participants receive syphilis medication. The Draft Board withdrew their request after receiving notification from the

Public Health Service of the study. Penicillin began being used as a cure for syphilis in 1943 and study participants were again excluded.

The Tuskegee Study stopped in 1972 with the reporting of associated press reporter Peter Buxton. From 1966 until 1972 Peter Buxton a venereal disease reporter had attempted to raise the issue to stop the study due to ethics violations and gross breach of institutional compliances of the federal government and Tuskegee. Despite Peter Buxton's presentations, the Tuskegee Study was still ongoing when the news received nationwide attention in the countries newspapers.

In 1976 historian James Jones interviewed John Heiler, director of the venereal disease unit of Public Health Service from 1943 until 1948. James Jones reported the most outrageous thing John Heiler spoke of during the interview was the status of the men participating in the study did not warrant any sort of ethical debate, and those studied are not patients, rather they are clinical material, not sick people.

The responsibility of the governing management of the study should have had the responsibility to receive the consent of the participants and to provide the needed care and treatment for a successful recovery.

There lies a vast difference to pre World War II America and the present. Human beings and the dignity toward ethics of 2010 had no rigidity in the ethical encyclopedia of the 1930s. Racial issues presented a paramount stamp on the minds, hearts and ethics of White America in the 1930s.

The Tuskegee studies provided valuable information of the ravages of syphilis, how the disease manifests itself in untreated humans. Even though this information and data led to the successful treatment of syphilis, the ethics and behavior of the Public Health Service and Tuskegee is horrendous and inhuman, a gross violation to the dignity of human society.

Evident today are the effects generated by the Tuskegee Syphilis study. Health-based community personnel report mistrust among African American communities. The Dallas Urban League's spokesperson Alpha Thomas has reported before the National Commission on Aids many African American people don't trust hospitals or other community health care providers because of the Tuskegee experiment.

A survey conducted by The Southern Christian Leadership Conference polled 1056 African American church members found 34% of respondents believed AIDS is an artificial virus

82

to further persecute and imprison African Americans in disease for further research. Other findings of this poll showed 35% believed AIDS and its associated research is a form of genocide. Another poll showed 44% believe AIDS is not a legitimate virus and the government is not revealing all associated truth concerning it and its research. Living in the 21st century presents its own set of circumstances concerning racial profiling. A person living in 2010 has the ability to reflect back on history and yet still be appalled at the conduct of researchers, which went on. Optimistically speaking a person living in 2010 would not conduct such a gross study, which inflicts such pain and agony on its victims.

The prevalent mindset of the medical community prior to World War II and During World War II seems archaic to the present medical community. To say simply an individual would never perform such an act of cruelty and breach of human ethics is shallow at best. An individual cannot simply place his or her beliefs into the past and systematically conclude an outcome would have been different.

George Washington stated those who do not learn from history will be prone to repeat it (Washington, 2008). Today's society believes humanity learns from intrusions and ethics violations such as the Tuskegee Study and associated research. Dr. Alexander Fleming formally made his experiments about penicillin to the medical world in 1929 as a result of luck and hard work, when Dr. Alexander Fleming accidentally knocked a pile of Petri dishes containing bacteria into a cleaning solution.

Syphilis is a dangerous venereal disease, which over time can ravage the human body and have serious and painful outcomes. The discovery of penicillin was of luck and hard work. Penicillin; a discovery, which could have averted the Tuskegee study, and brought about a cure to the participants of the Tuskegee Study plagued by syphilis, a pharmaceutical discovery commonly prescribed today. The Tuskegee Study; a sadistic tragedy, a cesspool of mistrust and betrayal, a catalyst for human ethics and ethical reform had its cure transpire the very same year of 1928.

"References"

Foster, C. (2001). The ethics of medical research on humans, Cambridge, United Kingdom: The Press syndicate of the University of Cambridge.

Jones, J. (1981).

Bad blood, New York Free Press. (n.d.).
Psycnet. Retrieved 1-10-2010 from
http://psycnet.apa.org.
BlogSpot. (2008). George Washingtons blog.
Retrieved 1-9-2010 from
http://georgewashingtons.blogspot.com

Those who suffered during this study will forever be changed. Their families will forever be impacted. They and others may never understand why these events transpired, but they did. They did, right here in the United States of America at the same time Hitler was persecuting the Jewish people.

Everyone today benefits from these atrocities. Does this make them right? Of course not, but we all have at one point of our lives benefited from the outcomes of this study and from the advances in medicine stemming from it and the healing powers of Penicillin. I am in no way attempting to present any solution to what happened here. I also am not trying to single out African American Men, nor am I attempting to try and give them any sort of advice or council. It is just a paper I wrote for a class. When I began my research, it moved me to tears. It moved me to examine my own heart and soul for my own sins. I read back over this paper and realize how a lot of it parallels my own life.

I look at the mindsets of those who conducted this study and can see how they viewed certain people. I notice so many parallels in those who conducted this experiment, to the Hitler Germans and certain mentalities to people like Marion Knox. Those might seem to be harsh words, however the actions perpetrated and the documented answers ring true.

Knox did not care about me nor did he care about my family. He cared about an outcome, which coincided with his philosophy. Knox was bound and determined to make my family and others fit into his preconceived mold. In the next chapter I will present information gathered from other families, which would produce the same set of questions, and produced the same outcomes.

I included this paper I wrote because I want to address the issue of Ethics and doing the ethical thing always. Why does a person like Marion Knox and others do what he or she does? Why would they continue to practice and teach something, which always ends up in broken homes? This is the prevailing question. Now along with this comes the question on its heels; what possible motive would he have for continuing to do and teach the things he does?

From what I have gathered from the legal counsel, which represents Marion Knox, there are people out there who have benefited from his therapy. I will go on the record right now and say I have been investigating this now for almost 3 years. Teila Tankersley my co-author has been helping me investigate all of this for almost a year now. We have not had any one person step forth and comment on how they have been helped.

We have however, found dozens of people who have had their homes wrecked, relationships broken, been incarcerated for things they did not do, myself included. Nearly every month brings a new story from someone influenced by Knox. Those stories lead us to others they know who have suffered the same way, had their homes shattered, marriages ending in divorce, and relationships with children and parents destroyed.

This question along with the others will lead us on through this book. Why would someone continue to practice something if the outcome would bring devastation to lives, cause insurmountable hurt, and change the course of human lives forever from the path they were set on? As I wrote in my paper, the whole Tuskegee Study was so atrocious of an act on the civil rights of African American Men during the 20's, 30's 40's. It is hard to understand why no one stopped the study! The conclusions I draw from my own research paper have led me to make some decisions in my own life.

Those decisions are the way I view my life at this stage of the game. It is not for me to try and understand why the events happened in my life. They did happen, and there is nothing I or anyone else can do to change what happened. I am becoming ever increasingly aware of the fact my life will never be the same as it was. At one point I led an average American life. The next minute I found myself in jail staring prison time in my face. A few months' later charges were dismissed, my family is torn to shreds and I have a record. The impact of this whole saga has effected three generations of my family.

Then the state of Oregon gets involved and says, "Even though your criminal charges were dropped we are still going to investigate you because of allegations." Three months later after a hearing, a psychosexual examination, and a polygraph test, a judge ruled the accusations were unfounded and were not proven beyond preponderance, and dismissed the case. Then I had to wait for another year for my record to be expunged during which time I was unable to secure a job because of the charges filed against me.

This I have determined: no amount of resentment, bitterness, hatred, revenge, or retaliation will make me, others, or those who perpetrated the acts against me change. I have a favorite saying, I post it where I can, when I can, and quote it to whomever I can whenever I can. It goes like this, "The difference between the words bitter and better is the 'I', when I focus on the 'I' I will be bitter, when I focus on the "E" as in everyone else, I will be better."

In trying to make sense of it all, I choose to be a better person. You may ask, Is this easy? No, it is not easy at all. Do I have moments and feelings when I want revenge, to hate, and to retaliate? Yes of course I do, I am human and I have feelings, emotions, and it hurts. It hurts a lot. Many nights go by where I cry myself to sleep. I miss my family life and especially my children. Through it all, I feel my life has been set on a new course. I so often have said to those closest to me, "I feel like I am in a high-speed car, and I am not the driver. I am just the passenger."

Most of us have seen the familiar poster where there are two sets of footprints in the sand and then there is only one. As the poster says,

"Lord, I know you are always with me, hence the two sets of footprints in the sand, but I noticed in the hardest times of my life there were only one set. Why did you leave me Lord during those times? To which the Lord replied, 'My child I am with you always and will never leave you. Those times in your life when you noticed only one set of footprints was not when I left you. It was when I carried you through your greatest trials.'"

My admonition to all out there whom have chosen to read this book, (and I am humbled by this decision) is if you have suffered a great injustice, as hard as it may seem, as hard as it may feel at times to overcome, as hard as it may be to understand your injustice, go on with life.

Determine within yourselves to be a better person, and not a bitter person. Take your hurt, your pain and let it strengthen you. Hopefully most of you will, but sad to say some of you will not. There is a plan for your life, a destiny awaits you. As you step out into the unknown, into your fear, into your hurt, a great strength will come.

There will be an insurmountable, overwhelming peace, which will help you go on. It will encompass your heart, mind, and soul. Forgive, and lead a productive life. Let your better life touch others, and let your better life help set others free. I awoke one morning in December 2010 with the thought of asking Teila to help me write this book. Soon after, her words to me were, "I have this great peace Steve, as you tell me your story." My friends, I know this peace. This peace goes far beyond my comprehension. I knew then and there I had made the right decision in asking for her help.

Just as Tuskegee was a huge injustice to the African American community, so I feel my happenings, arrest and sudden isolation in life, were a great injustice to me and to those I love and cherish in this life. I cannot change this; instead I choose to help people through it, to make my life count for the good. To help see people not suffer in any way I can and if the Lord permits me, to lead others to a place where they find peace. A place where they can come to in their lives to find the strength, the peace and contentment to live productive lives, which can touch someone I may not be able to.

Drop of water by Jani Ravas

Chapter Five
The ethical thing to do.

"The worst prison would be a closed heart to the needs of others." Pope John Paul II

Here I sit writing this book, and I take into consideration the subject of Tuskegee and my own story and what I just said, ethics. I believe words build bridges into undiscovered lands; lands, which have waters not chartered, and unexplored regions teaming with a wealth of information. All of our lives are a journey. Each one of are on our own journey. This is why I am learning to not compare myself with anybody else. We are in this world for something, which is greater than ourselves. I ask myself over and over again; Steve, what is the ethical thing for you to do? I realize no amount of work or anything I may do can change anything. I sit here and I ponder about 13 year old Cari Lightner, who was killed by a hit-and-run driver as she walked down a suburban street in Fair Oaks, California in the early 1980's.

"I promised myself on the day of Cari's death; I would fight to make this needless homicide count for something positive in the years ahead," Candy Lightner, Cari's mother later wrote.

Ms. Lightner was appalled at the leniency of the sentence given to the repeat offender of driving while intoxicated (DWI), it outraged Lightner the man who killed her daughter was given a lenient sentence. It led her to make some decisions, which would affect this Country forever.

Lightner then organized Mothers Against Drunk Drivers. The name was later changed to Mothers Against Drunk Driving. The object of her organization was to raise public awareness of the serious nature of drunk driving and to promote tough legislation against this crime.

Lightner appeared on major television

shows, spoke before the US Congress, addressed professional and business groups, and worked tirelessly for years to change public attitudes, modify judicial behavior, and promote tough new legislation. She left MADD in 1985.

She has since stated MADD "has become far more neo-prohibitionist than she had ever wanted or envisioned … she went on to say she didn't start MADD to deal with alcohol. "I started MADD to deal with the issue of drunk driving" she stated. She was led to deal with the people behind the bottle. The person and people like the driver who hit and killed her daughter; who are not willing to be responsible for their own decisions.

Candy Lightner is a recipient of the President's Volunteer Action Award, an honorary doctorate in humanities, and public service. She and was the subject of a made-for-television movie, "Mothers Against Drunk Drivers: the Candy Lightner story." She is the co-author (with Nancy Hathaway) of 'Giving Sorrow Words.' For her work, Lightner was commended by President Ronald Reagan himself. Her vision was to create an awareness of the dangers of drunk driving, which has changed history. This Candy Lightner felt, was the ethical thing for her to do.

I am not attempting to create my own organization. I am however bent on exposing lies and misinterpretations, which can cause unneeded and undue pain and suffering of others.

We can never fully know how many lives have been changed and redirected because of the efforts of Candy Lightner. How many people have changed their minds and not driven while intoxicated because of her efforts? It appalls me a man like Marion Knox can continue to do what he does.

As Teila Tankersley and I began to co-author this book, more and more people began to step forward with testimonies like my own. Every day we discover something, which astonishes us.

I recall one instance prior to September 2008, I came home and my wife was reading some sort of book. At the time I paid it very little attention, as she read a lot, but one book in particular stood out. It was a book, which highlighted symbols and pictures, which were supposedly associated with the Masons and the Occult.

My wife said to me, "Steve, look at this book." Later in the evening she came out of our bedroom and she was terrified beyond belief. She had in her hand this same book. I discovered it

was a book written by Dr. Cathy Burns called;
"Masonic and Occult Symbols Illustrated." She
showed me a picture in the book.

"This is the picture, which was on the lodge my
father belonged to when I was a child."

She went on to say, "I remember my dad would
take me to his meetings. I never went inside with
him; he always made us stay in the car."

A few weeks later I came home from
work. I remember vividly the night; we had a
horrible rainstorm earlier in the day and the
power had gone off a few times. I came in and
she was sitting there staring at this book.

"Steve," she said, "I have been sick all day."

What's wrong I asked.

"I talked to Marion today and I told him about
the lodge symbol I showed you. He helped me
discover when I was three years old and I went to
a human sacrifice this lodge was conducting.
They sacrificed a human baby and I was there,
and they made me drink the baby's blood
afterward."

I could not believe what I was hearing. I told her
"no way,"

She replied this to me, "No, I am sure of it. I
don't remember it happening but after talking
with Marion, I believe it did happen and I was
there, I feel like I am going to puke."

I looked at the book and kind of flipped through the pages. "Where did you get this," I asked her

"From Marion," she replied.

She was absolutely torn up at this; I did not believe it and I tried to talk her out of it. She continued to affirm this did indeed happen to her.

Here's the key to this whole line of B.S. Marion Knox fed her. She told me she did not have any memories of it, but she knew it happened because when she met with Marion Knox she had this overwhelming feeling this had indeed happened.

Now I am going to say right here and right now if this sort of thing takes place in a person's life they are going to remember it, period, end of discussion. No regressed memories.

I knew Marion Knox was a total lunatic from almost the get go. Later a friend in whom I was confiding in right before I was removed from my home telephoned Marion Knox. He had no knowledge of what Marion Knox had told my wife. I am going to include right here a copy of his email, which he sent to my attorney,

"This has been sent to your attorney.
My name is Xxxxxx and I'm writing in regards to my conversation with Marion Knox.

I only spoke with him one time of any length. I told Mr. Knox my Grandfather was a Mason. Upon hearing this, the questions from Mr. Knox became what I felt to be very "leading in nature." He asked if someone was wearing some ceremonial, ritual robe. I was also led to believe I killed a baby and drank the blood.

After talking with him I felt violated and it affected my emotional state. After our conversation I had to pray and ask God for forgiveness as well as cleansing.
Let me know if you need anything else"

----- Original Message -----

Sent: Wednesday, February 11, 2009 12:41:55 PM GMT -08:00 US/Canada Pacific
Subject: Marion Knox

I have since been in distant contact with this individual.

As people began to come forward when we began writing our book, we started to discover some interesting things. Knox's questions and his "leading of questions" appear to be more commonplace. The man is completely obsessed with the notion of sodomy. At one point while talking on the phone with him and my wife he told us he believes over 90% of all living people have at one time been sodomized. This is a pretty staggering statement.

Now I would go out on a limb at this point and ascertain most people do not sit around and wonder and ponder the idea of sodomy. I don't think a majority of the average public at large contemplates this on any given level. I am not a Mason, nor do I have any members in my family who are members of the Masons and Eastern Star. But as stated above, this man's train of thought and questions is all the same when it comes to those who have family members involved with the Masons. Here is another line of questions with another family recovering from Marion Knox's therapy.

I sent the before mentioned email to this other family and she responded in this way to me.

From: X & X X@bendbroadband.com>
To: Steve Skotko <steveskotko@yahoo.com>;
Teila Tankersley <progitive37@yahoo.com>
Sent: Sun, December 19, 2010 5:02:49 PM
Subject: Re: who else?
Hi all....I wanted to get a little more specific regarding Xxxxxx's comment. I posted right on his letter with my own 'bold' words.
(The original email)

This was sent to your att.

My name is Xxxxx and I'm writing in regards to my conversation with Marion Knox.

I only spoke with him one time of any length.

I told Mr. Knox my Grandfather was a Mason. Upon hearing this, the questions became what I felt to be very leading.

Yes, he focused on Masons and the Occult. At one point, I asked if our daughter shouldn't come up with the information and MK shouldn't be the first to talk about the blood, death, locked in a box, sodomy, etc. He said he knew where it was leading and this speeded up the process if he asked leading questions!

He asked if someone was wearing some ceremonial ritual robe. I was also led to believe I killed a baby and drank the blood.

Yes, drinking blood and death were all part of it for everyone we knew who was MK's client.

After talking with him I felt violated and it affected my emotional state.

After our conversation I had to pray and ask God for forgiveness as well as cleansing.

Let me know if you need anything else

To which I Steve asked this person the following question

So everyone who told MK they had a Mason in the family, he took down this road with human sacrifice and drinking the blood, is this your assessment?

To which they responded,

"Hi Steve,

Yes. There's no question about this! MK had a specific agenda!
When we were involved with MK, we were amazed all his clients had the same prognosis. Our daughter (and we would, too, at first) would sit in on another client's session with MK.
I remember one gal, xxxxx xxxxxx, who went over the river and through the woods on dramatic things she had been through. Sure enough, the next session our daughter would remember the same things had happened to her, too!!! Now, we all know those things DID NOT AND COULD NOT have happened! "
Sincerely, xxxxx

Now I Steve can attest to these comments. At first when we met Marion Knox we had no idea this all would lead to these types of questions. With me having been a Catholic, Knox did not try to ask me questions as he asked these other people. He propositioned me with a whole separate line of questions concerning catholic priests, especially Jesuit priests. He tried to convince me, I had been sodomized by a catholic priest after he had learned I had been an altar boy. When I said I had not been abused in any way he did not believe me. He simply dismissed it. He tried to convince me I had suppressed the memories because they were so horrible. Knox did however, persist through my wife and then eventually to my children without my knowledge I had indeed been sodomized as a child. Since I had been sodomized I would have had to abuse my children in the form of sodomy, because I would not be able to suppress these urges.

At one point he had them believing and they probably still do, they, my children, were abused by both sides of their family. He called it the "double whammy!"

No thoughts, discussions, or "overwhelming" feelings ever existed in my family before we met Marion Knox. This was what life was like. Leading my family in life was hard enough, running a business, and all the events parents do with children. Now, at the same time for over 5 years I had to deal with this insane, lunatic person influencing my family on these ridiculous, disturbing, and outlandish beliefs!

Sad to say my wife bought it; hook, line, and sinker, after over twenty years of marriage, which included numerous sicknesses, tragedies, and times of prosperity. I remember at one point when my oldest son was a baby having to resuscitate him when he stopped breathing because of an allergic reaction to a childhood immunization. Those were times of "family." Those times brought us closer to each other, yet this madness perpetrated by Knox had a way of twisting it to make my wife believe it was all a lie. She began to believe it was all a subconscious plan I had to keep my children alive to propagate the demonic influence in my family heritage.

I mean, man, where did he get this stuff from, it's crazy? This line of thinking is not normal, yet he relentlessly pursued it. Later at one point I asked him, "So do you really believe 90% of all people are walking around in an altered state of mind because they all at some point had been sodomized, and a majority of them do not remember it happening?"

"Oh yes, I do, he exclaimed!"

Then he looked at me and asked me "Do you believe Doris or I have ever been sodomized?"

I thought, not so much about the question, but about the look in his eyes when he asked me the question. "Yes I do," I replied.
To which he said "Well as near as we can figure, there is no evidence this has ever occurred in mine or Doris' life."
How convenient, everyone else has been sodomized, except for him and his wife!

Upon interviewing Marion Knox, Ron Patton asked Marion Knox this question.
RP: Have there been any repercussions, like threats on your life for helping Illuminati Rothschild survivors?
MK: Virtually none. The Lord has helped me to not be afraid and as long as he wants me to be alive and untouched, he won't allow anyone to get to me.

I found an interesting quote it goes like this "I believe today t my conduct is in accordance with the will of the Almighty Creator. Who says I am not under the special protection of God?

I soon will tell you the author of this quote, to some it may surprise you, to others it will amaze. I have determined the ethical thing for me to do is to expose this stuff for what it really it. There have been many families, lives, and individuals torn up by this sort of teaching.

Mine is not an isolated incident. These teachings find root in many Pentecostal church denominations in the world. The concept of demonic possession is prevalent in the teachings and doctrines of many churches. It is amazing to me the ones who claim to have this special power or gift, also have the smallest churches and congregations. One would think if this was such a truth and such a key for personal peace and wholeness many would be flocking for help. Civilization has seen many such "miracle happenings," and when they do they all flock to get it.

Produce a bottle of water and put it on the market claiming it can restore your youth and have one documented proof, and you won't be able to keep the stuff on the shelves.

People like my family and others are sincerely searching for something, which will help them. Every person or family member who has faced a medical crisis during his or her lifetime has at one point hoped for an immediate cure; a process, which would deter any sort of painful or prolonged convalescence. People who are sick want to be well. People suffering from depression want to be able to not be depressed any longer. People with Cancer will do everything they can to be cured. People in need of a transplant will get desperate for the needed organ. Some will traverse onto the highway of the black market to secure their needed organ.

Stem cell treatment is a very controversial subject. People will trade their ethical values to secure those stem cells in a chance they will produce their needed cure. My goal is not to personally prosper from this book or any lawsuit or spin offs of them. I simply want this insanity to stop.

People will always search for answers. This is what makes us unique beings on this planet; the will to learn and gain knowledge. What none of us possesses is the right to abuse or misuse any amount of power or authority we may have. We have no right to freely exercise the things we may benefit from over others who seem to be subservient or weaker than ourselves.

Earlier in this chapter I stated a quote. I felt this quote went along really well with my train of thought in this chapter. I want to take time here and put some other quotes down from the same individual.

"All propaganda has to be popular and has to accommodate itself to the comprehension of the least intelligent of those whom it seeks to reach."

"As a Christian I have no duty to allow myself to be victimized, but I have the duty to be a fighter for truth and justice."

"By the skillful and sustained use of propaganda, one can make a people see even heaven as hell or an extremely wretched life as paradise."

"He alone, who owns the youth, gains the future"
"Great Liars are also great magicians."
"I use emotion for the many and reserve reason for the few."
"Create a lie, make it a big one. Tell people over and over and they will eventually believe it to be truth."
"If you tell a big enough lie and tell it frequently enough it will be believed."

When I found these quotes it amazed me how through reading the interviews posted by Ron Patton and Elena Freeland this individual, Marion Knox, had stated similar things. I began to draw parallels, and discover patterns. This led me to my ethical decision. My decision is as follows.

"I have lived a good life. I loved one woman in this life and dedicated my life to her and my children. Contrary to her beliefs, I never

107

had an affair during our marriage. It does not matter to me what she or other may believe.

This is the truth. I will stand upon this truth. When I said I do, I meant it, and remained faithful to her. I always respected her and even though I feel she made certain wrong decisions regarding divorce, I never agreed with them nor did I have the chance to get her to change her mind, mostly because a restraining order held me at bay. My signature is on no divorce paperwork. It was her decision. I was not present at the divorce hearing, because I did not believe in it so I did not participate in it."

My original quote I used earlier in this chapter was this

"I believe today my conduct is in accordance with the will of the Almighty Creator. Who says I am not under the special protection of God?"

I will do all in my power to stop this man, his teaching and his influence, and yet not violate my own set of ethic's, I simply want to tell my story.

-Oh by the way all those quotes I used in this chapter were from one man as I said. The man was Adolf Hitler!

Narrow Hallway by John Hi-Fi

Chapter Six

Clinging to hope (Finding my way through the
long and narrow hall)

"Once you choose hope, anything's possible."
Christopher Reeve

When Teila and I started off on this
journey to put my experiences into words, she
asked me to find a picture we could affix to the
original article she wrote and posted on the
internet. The first thing, which popped into my
head, was of a long road through a dessert. I
thought of the scene in the movie "Forest Gump"

109

when he was doing his running. When he had finally stopped he was positioned in the middle of the dessert with rock formations in the distance. I then thought of a long hallway with no windows and no doors, which disappeared into nothing. I feel like I am on a long road, in which you cannot see the end. Or, I am walking down a long hallway, which has no windows or doors and you cannot see the end. Most of the time it is difficult to put into words what I am experiencing as I don't know exactly what it is I am experiencing at certain given times.

Whoosh, I feel better, I said it. One day I found myself in the middle of a desert and I seemed to have no recollection of how I got there. I could see pillars in my life in the distance. At first I thought they might be goals I was heading toward. I then realized they weren't goals at all. They were past accomplishments.

For a period of time after my ordeal began, by the way I call it 'the ordeal' because I cannot think of anything better to call it. Oh I could, but I am attempting to keep things and my wording as decent as I can. I can find all kinds of adjectives or colorful metaphors, but to purposely use them I believe is wrong. If one slips out now and again I can live with it.

110

So my ordeal begins and I am smack in the middle of this desert. Forrest Gump had it better than me in he had a following of people who admired and supported him. I had no one. For about one day I had absolutely nobody there. If you don't think this sounds so bad then I pray the good Lord will permit you to see, feel and experience one similar day in your life. Like I already had said, the first person I called on the telephone was my mother. Not because she was my mother, but because she was my mother, I had wronged her and my family in Ohio and needed to make things right.

In reality to get through this endless hallway, which was just beginning and clinging to hope, the first thing I did was reconcile myself with my Core Value [1]. This is an interesting thing; you're Core Value. We all have one, yet most of us do not realize or even know there is such a thing as a Core Value. Core Value is present in all humans at birth. It is the instinctual self-worth, which makes newborns presume their emotional needs will be met by their mother.

If you think of it, a fetus is in a warm, secure place with all of its needs met. This is established in each and every life. Throughout life, Core Value tells us how important, valuable, loving, and loveable we are It forms the

111

foundation of personal security, well-being, self-esteem, competence, creativity, and power.

Core Value is the deepest experience of the self. It is the human soul. It is clear awareness, which no problem, behavior, or event can reduce your value as a person. It is a deep feeling you are O.K., even if certain behavior needs to change. It is the deepest feeling of self, which no one can ever take away or deny. When we are in touch with our Core Value we can do no wrong. It is a moral compass in our life.

Core Value is the source of deep choice, change, and the sense of self. Without Core Value, we would have no understanding of Value, quality, morality, or religion. Everything we value comes from Core Value. This is exactly what happens when you are abused. Abuse separates you from your Core Value. It does not steal it. Nothing can steal it. You are merely separated from it. You are standing in the middle of a desert looking around, totally separated, totally isolated from the rest of the world.

At times during my ordeal I have felt literally like I was clinging for hope. Not only as I stated did I lose all my possessions in life, my family and my dignity; and for a time, I lost my hope. Hope is a powerful emotion. Hope has kept people alive, which were trapped. Hope has sustained entire populations of people, even when inevitable death stared them in the face.

Through everything, providence has been upon my life, providence has been my brother. There has been a supernatural blessing at work in my life, which has sustained me. I believe God sustained me because I had been in contact with my Core Value. This ordeal merely separated me from my Core Value. I know in my heart my calling at this stage of my life is to write these words in this book.

You are reading this book and you may have been abused in some way. In some cases we are not abused by someone or something directly, we could be abused indirectly. We may have a loved one or a friend who has suffered something terrible in life or maybe even a friend who has been beaten by a spouse or their significant other.

It can be someone close to us who are dealing with alcoholism or has someone they love who is. It may not just be this; it can be any sort of abuse. You sit back and watch as he or she is dealing with this situation. You want to be a friend, a confidant to them. You listen and support them. When they leave your presence you feel drained, dirty and exhausted. They phone you and just want someone to "vent" to. Figuratively speaking they vomit all over you. In this way you are abused, because they are. You are abused because you have chosen to enter into the abuse with them. Unless you get this person the help they need or can offer them some sort of reprieve from their pain, it is going to continue for them. You cannot say anything, which will help them because Core Value is not about words.

You have been abused and you are saying to yourself "this is me, this is me!" Acknowledging this is the first step for you. Hear the words you are thinking, "This is me, or maybe this is I."

Core Value is so deep and early an experience it does not work in words. Internal images activate Core Value. Those words you are thinking are your Core Value speaking to you, it comes from your soul. This is why there is no words, which someone can speak to you to comfort you. You need to connect back to your Core Value.

Abuse begins the separation from your Core Value. Anger, resentment and all the others finish you off. Taking medications only help relieve the pain of being separated from your Core Value. They won't reconnect you with your Core Value. Many people spend their whole lives in the attempt to reconnect with their Core Value and fail.

The primary image of Core Value is a deep, bright, warm light. Secondary images of Core Value can seem realistic, like an accelerated sunrise piercing the dark night and beautifully illuminating the world. Or they can seem abstract, like shimmering colors in swirling patterns. Core Value can have sound, like birds chirping at dawn. They can have motion, like a sense of movement through color and space. They can have warmth and light or seem cool and dim. They can excite you or calm you, please or focus you. Your Core Value images must come from deep inside you and make you feel as important, valuable, and deserving as anyone else in the world.

The above explanation of Core Value is something I learned over a period of time and an extensive court appointed anger management class. It helped me learn this and how to reconnect with my Core Value. I have witnessed miraculous things, which come at the most convenient times to keep me encouraged and nourished in life.

These small miracles helped me reconnect to my Core Value. I will never forget being housed at the Lynn County, Oregon jail for three days. As I was entering I asked the guard if I could have a bible, he reluctantly agreed. For three days in my cell all I did was sleep and read. I would read until my eyes were ready to pop out. I would then sleep and then awake and read again. What did I read in the bible for 3 days? I read the Psalms. No matter what religious persuasion you are, or even if you are not, you should read the Psalms. You need to have it on your read list at least once in your lifetime.

The book of Psalms opens the window of your soul. It goes into great detail at times and covers any mental state or emotional state you may ever face. It brings words of encouragement, strength, hope, fortitude, and promises of divine intervention in life. Reading Psalms will help you reconnect you with your Core Value. One thing I firmly stand on and one thing I absolutely believe is "God sees all." He takes note of everything, which happens in our lives and He keeps real good books!

This is me, my Core Value. Oh, I know at times we don't feel this way. Sometimes it is hard to feel and to believe God is indeed watching over us. Our feelings can lie to us, most of the time they do. Things are not always as they appear and usually in our darkest moments in life the supernatural is at work. Life is not fair; then again who ever made the statement it should be fair. You must realize since the only thing you can ultimately control is you, so the issues in your life start with you. I am so thankful I realized early in my situation the root issues were really about me. I have been able to get a handle on the "fair issues of life."

In saying all of this I now want to ask you the questions I asked myself. Where is the book or instruction manual entitled "The fair rules of life" located? Who authored such a book? Where is it housed? What is its library of congress number? My friend there isn't one. It does not exist. The sooner you understand the sooner you can get over it. Whatever "it" may be in your life or whoever "it" is in your life! The thing I decided early on was I would not carry resentment. Resentment will further separate me from my Core Value. Resentment had to go!

The following was written by Toni Morrison. Toni is a Nobel and Pulitzer Prize winning American novelist, editor, and professor. Her novels are known for their epic themes, vivid dialogue, and richly detailed black characters. Among her best known novels are "The Bluest Eye, Song of Solomon and Beloved." I have left the content of this statement intact in its original

117

form as the author wrote it. I am sorry if some of the words offend any of you.

<u>"Wanna fly; you got to give up the 'shit,' which weighs you down."</u>
"Our old 'shit' is so precious to us. We tenderly harbor our old resentments like pets and periodically throw them pieces of fresh flesh to keep them alive. We nurture our anger. We don't do anything to work it through or let it go! We just hang on and nurture it. Then we wonder why we feel so stuck and held back in our lives! When we hold onto old 'shit' it weighs us down, it is as if our feet are stuck in fresh tar! There comes a time, in which we can see it doesn't really matter what someone has done to us, our holding onto it is hurting us and not them.

If we want to heal we had best take our old 'Shit' and fertilize the flowers"

THE ONLY WAY TO GROW IS TO LET GO!

Let go friend, let go and quit carrying the "Shit." I had to let go. It has been determined most physical ailments are connected to feelings of resentment, anger, and bitterness. Bitterness is a terrible poison in the kettle called "Life." It will kill you, put you on drugs, and squash the life out

118

of you. Bitterness will "dry your bones."

The ill-health effects of anger come not from frequency and intensity or how often you get angry and how angry you get but with duration or how long it lasts. Unhealthy levels of anger are those, which last longer than a couple of minutes. The anger levels in conflictive circumstances give you a 5-7 times greater chance of dying before the age of 50.

I had so many injustices hit me one right after the other. I have already told you some of the things, which transpired in my life. I have not even scratched the surface. I am going to share more on anger in a bit. My anger at my situation was not going to be dealt with immediately but over a period of time and a bit down the road. For a while I felt justified in my anger.

Yes I did of course; I was wronged! I was burned in life and I had every justification to feel so and let the world know it. The Problem was the world did not want to know it; which was my anger. People were interested in my story, but not my anger and certainly not my resentment.

So in essence to get a better hand on the rope in my life, which we have termed "clinging for hope," I had to deal with myself. I dealt with my failures. When I did, all the other things I would deal with and get over, lined up in perfect fashion like a regimented military troop awaited my orders to be dismissed.

The first thing I did was reconcile to the ones I had wronged, and to the ones I was able to. Just like I have said; first was my family. I then reconciled with my good friend Gale who at the time was living in Florida. Gale instantly forgave me and as he stated, "There is nothing to forgive, I love you brother."

Since this first phone call he has been my very closest Confidant. Right from the beginning he stopped me in a conversation and said to me, "I am going to ask you this once and never again, Did you do it?" I said "no." and the case was closed and he has stood behind me ever since. He and a few others, and I am talking like counting those others on one hand, have done me the dignity of asking me first without drawing conclusions. This was a huge thing because with all the accusations, restraining orders, and rumors, most of those individuals floating around in my life just believed the accusations and came to the conclusions; "since I was accused it must be true." Does this sound like sound mature advice you would want to give someone else to have your life judged by?

Hey here is another one for you "Do unto

others as you would have them do unto you!"
This quote or a variation of it is practically in
every religion in the world. Christian, Jewish,
Muslim, Buddhism, Hinduism, Pagan, Agnostic,
Mother Earth and la-de-da-de-da all have this
somewhere in their creed or doctrine! So I have
determined it was not the circumstance, which
associates of mine turned up their noses at, it was
just good little ole' me!

Yep, this is what it was and this is what I
had to deal with first on my way back to sanity. It
was ME! It was "I"! Yes it was and nobody else.
I was standing there in the smack dab middle of
the "Desert I". The abuse I suffered and the
treatment I received placed me there.

The "Desert I" is a very lonely place.
Everyone on this planet goes there at some point;
most of us go there often in our lives. Many deal
with it and conquer it. In order to deal with it and
conquer it, one has to cross it. I was looking to
take this long grueling road, which appears to go
nowhere. For many, they just can't deal with it
and just turn around and simply go back to those
monuments I spoke of, which are their past
achievements.

In my circumstance and in the
circumstances of people suffering from the abuse
of others, there is nothing to go back to. I refused

to just agree to exist and live in the "Desert I". I refused the help of Alcohol, drugs (both prescription and non prescription) and the advice of Constituents and Comrades (remember those guys). I would not be content to live in the "Desert I". For some, they can maintain a pretty good existence there in "Desert I"

The things never to get restored in the "Desert I" in your life are your dignity, self worth, and self respect (I think you get it now). Once I dealt with the reality I was dwelling in the "Desert I", I then dealt with the resentment and the Anger both present and thriving in the "Desert I".

On the other side of the "Desert I" lay my Core Value and I was and am determined to get back to it. Yes, if you are content to dwell and sustain yourself in your own "Desert I" you will never reconnect with your Core Value again. You will never truly be healed. While dwelling in the "Desert I" there is not much growing there to nourish you with. Anger, resentment, and bitterness all flourish and grow gangbusters in the "Desert I". You will never be nourished by these things.

There is no rain in the "Desert I". Anger, resentment, and bitterness don't need rain to grow.. Anger is the animal, which lives in the

"Desert I". Anger is the ruling animal. Like a Lion in the jungle, Anger is king of "Desert I". Anger is the meat; it is the protein you can sustain your existence on in the "Desert I".

Anger feeds on the vegetable or grain, which grows in the "Desert I" and this is Resentment. Anger is able to live, survive and grow by consuming Resentment and so too are you. I lived in the "Desert I" for a brief stint. Bitterness is another herb, which grows there. Bitterness gives flavor to Anger and Resentment. It makes it easier to consume. It also needs no water to live, grow and flourish. Resentment is flavored with the Bitterness growing around it.

All three flourish there. So you see they are all happy there. They were all happy to be there with me as I existed and was living in the "Desert called I". I was miserable and lost. This is what I discovered about myself. This is what I dealt with to bring me hope to make it through.

Here is some stuff about resentment and anger. Long lasting levels of anger relate to the following;

1. The destruction of T-cells (depressing and immune system), if you are angry a lot, you probably have lots of little aches and pains; get colds and bouts of the flu.

2. You will develop Hypertension and the increased threat of stroke, heart disease, cancer, and a shortened life span.

3. The effects on the cognitive thought component are interesting. Many studies confirm the old saying about "being so mad you can't think straight," anger severely impairs all thought processes. These include; reality testing (did this really happen? Did I do this?), perception, learning and memory, problem solving, and creativity and performance competence [1].

Anything you do angry you can do better not being angry. Anger only hurts you. Then over time I dealt with resentment. Just like what was stated in the quote by Toni Morrison, I decided to quit carrying around my "shit" and I chose to fertilize the flowers.

It would have been so easy to just stay and live in the desert. I could have survived there in the "Desert I". I could have just blamed someone else, lived in anger, and existed.

Notes Chapter 6:

[1] Core Value used by permission from The Treatment Manual of the Compassion Workshop by Steven Stosny PhD, Copyright 1995.

The Pendulum

Chapter Seven
Details of the "Mengele" Pendulum

Authors note: In chapter 7, 8&9. I will be explaining and talking about Joseph Mengele. Mengele was a Nazi war criminal from World War II. It is for the benefit of those who may not know who Mengele was or as to what he experimented in. There has been a movement over the past few decades to not teach these historic issues in the schools, I want the reader to be fully aware of who he was.

The most intriguing thing of it all is with as much drama and hysteria, in which everything happened, it just went totally dormant. From late September of 2008 thru the end of November, nothing happened. No word came concerning any of the events or legal proceedings, it just fell silent.

As I spoke of before; November 27 was my 25th wedding anniversary and I spent it in a park in Salem, Oregon, feeding Thanksgiving dinner to the homeless. I wanted to do this. I decided to do something to help others. When I think back it is quite ironic this was my anniversary, it would fall on Thanksgiving Day.

During this period I felt thankful for nothing. I was staying in a small monthly hotel room when word came from my attorney on November 28, 2008.

"I just received and email indicating the DA was dismissing your case relating to sex abuse etc. There is still something out there
about an alleged restraining order violation, which we will need to deal with but otherwise things look well. I tried calling the number I had at home, but it had been disconnected. I'll talk with you next week.
Congrats!!!"

Now if this was not a pendulum, nothing was. All the grief, hurt, frustration, and heartache ended quickly, with an "email". Now don't take me wrong, I was grateful to have the charges dropped. The alleged restraining order violation occurred on the Friday evening I was released from jail. I went to my employee's house to retrieve my equipment. I was told at this time it was returned to my wife at my house. I left, and later this night I received a phone call from the Albany police to turn myself in because I had gone within 150 feet of my house. I had not and after a phone call from my attorney, I turned off the phone and went to sleep on a friends couch.

I like to use the word pendulum at this point, so I looked up the word "pendulum" here are a few definitions;
'A weight hung from a fixed point so it can swing freely back and forth under the influence of gravity,' and 'Something, which changes its direction or position regularly, often alternating between two extremes.'

Nothing made sense, I had no idea what was going on. The only thing I knew was they were dropping all the charges. This part of the ordeal was all over. It would be just a few weeks and I was off to travel to Ohio to be reunited with my family after 5 years of zero contact. For the moment the pendulum seemed to be allied with the armies of sanity. The battlefield my pendulum was on was sanity versus the insane.

When all of these events started happening I began to just function in life. When it was happening I thought I was handling it all very well. The best word I can muster to use for this period in my life was "numb." 6 months later I would look back and wonder how the heck I made it through all. Then 6 months later again I would think 'how did I make it.' Once I permanently moved to Ohio in September of 2009 my therapist would explain to me I was probably in shock. However, she was unable to make this determination since my visits were after the fact.

From all we could put together I was in shock. I then had a round with P.T.S.D. Post Traumatic Stress disorder takes place when someone faces a life threatening or life altering event. I don't believe I had this to the severity our combat troops would experience it. None the less I was traumatized and stressed so according to her I was feeling the effects of P.T.S.D..

I admit to you as you as you read these words, I was in an isolated place and in an isolated frame of mind. I spent many hours reflecting and closely examining my life. I was in the desert place. The "Desert I" as I like to call it.

I did not even know at the time it was a desert place. It was through much prayer, soul searching, and timely words from my confidant I would be able to figure out what was happening and how to begin to cope with things. The only true friend I had was Gale. We have spoken nearly every day for the last two and a half years by telephone. I have not seen him for three and a half years. But, He has been a constant source of encouragement during this time. He has supported me, cried with me, listened, and encouraged me. This is what a confidant is all about. These are the type of people I want surrounding me.

This period of time is probably the most difficult time to put into words what was happening. I was numb all over. I was in shock. I had no emotions so to speak of for long periods of time. Then, I would be flooded with a barrage of feelings and a salvo of emotions. Little things I would experience would trigger memories, which would unleash the onslaught of emotions. I had dreams so vivid of my children; I would awake to a bombardment of tears. I was definitely in survival mode and needed a direction in my life. I felt nothing. My soul was a bottomless pit, which would swallow up all the strength I could stir within myself. Not only did all of these things happen with my wife and children, but my business went in the tank. The newspaper printed the following blurb when I was arrested.

Public Safety Log
Posted: Wednesday, September 24, 2008 12:00 am |

People arrested are innocent unless proven otherwise in court. Initial charges often change as a case progress.

ALBANY POLICE
Arrest - Stephen John Skotko, 47, of Albany was arrested Tuesday on charges of sexual abuse and related offenses. Police said the alleged crimes took place a number of years ago and involved a victim, a girl known to Skotko, who was 8 to 14 at the time.

After this little article it was hard to function in what was left of my construction business. I would walk into a place where I had conducted business and I would know immediately who knew what had transpired in my life and to what conclusion they had drawn in their minds. On the other hand I would begin to discover the true character of people.

It took a number of months to begin to learn this. This was when individuals would begin to be weeded from my life. This process has continued to this day. I began to learn the true nature of those, which had been functioning in my life. Any ulterior motives would be unearthed.

When the ordeal began I was under contract to build a garage for my insurance agent at his personal residence. He terminated the contract while I was visiting the county jail. This was not really legal or ethical, but he did it nonetheless. As it turned out he was not really "on my side." Then his next move was to hire my employees after telling them I would not be getting out of jail any time soon.

It appears during my incarceration he telephoned detective Fairall who visited him at his place of business. During this visit the good detective informed him "I was going away for a very long time. (I have this testimony on recorded media as well from the contractor's board hearing)."

He used my materials and former crew of workers to complete his garage addition. Oh of course everyone always files a restraining order to make their case look good and this is exactly what he did. Then again at this particular moment in time, I was the bad guy again having been "accused." It was actually this man's wife who said she was afraid I would molest her kids, simply because of the accusations.

I am amazed at how easily our judicial system will approve a restraining order. Once in place you are barred for one year. It's another part of our judicial system, which was established for the good and protection of the people and easily abused by society. For this customer to finish his project he needed a building permit. He tried to use mine claiming it was his, but as the contractor it was mine. He even had a few inspections performed while it was under my name even though he illegally terminated our agreement.

The process of all of this ran its course over the next few months with a hearing before the Oregon Contractors Board in which they split the decision down the middle and I was required to refund about $2,000 to the customer. This total was basically my profits for the period of time I was actually on the job.

During this whole process he did not have a copy of his contract. During the hearing (which I possess of recorded copy of the proceedings) the customer presented a copy of the contract. He never had one for 3 months and then he possessed one at the hearing. He later stated he secured the contract from my house by way of my wife. He had my original copy of the contract at the hearing.

Oh yes going back to having a valid building permit, he secured this thru a former friend whom we will call "DC". They used my original paper work, my drawings I drew up to secure the new building permit. The original paper work was in only two places; on my computer and a hard copy filed with the city of Albany, Oregon, which was part of my file for the building permit I bought.

The new building permit paperwork was backdated. This would show compliance for the inspections, which were illegally done while the project was still under my name. His new building permit was backdated to before I was even arrested and still under contract.

To even add more insult to the whole drama of everything, "DC" completed the contract and building, was compensated for his efforts, and I believe he split the profit with my wife for her involvement in providing them with the contract.

The original contract was in my house because I could not take it when they filed the

134

restraining order on me to remove me from my home, which I never went back to. "DC" was a former friend and pastor of a church, which my family and I had attended for a short period of time. Originally it was his recommendation we meet Marion Knox.

I will tell you what; Peyton place could not top this whole scenario! This whole scenario took place during the time I was living in a hotel in Salem, Oregon waiting for the charges against me to be dismissed.

It was total mayhem; everything was being ripped and torn from under and around me. My life, business, and livelihood were being shredded away and I could do nothing about it. Upon later discussions with former victims of Marion Knox, we concluded this mayhem to be the norm. First they come in and just devastate your world with all kinds of accusations, arrest you, some end up in jail, and others do not.

Then come all the restraining orders because of course those of us accused are the bad men and everyone else needs to be protected. After this, everything just gets dismissed and thrown out of court. In the mean time my life is a wreck. This just did not happen to me. We have others stepping forward who will testify to the same set of circumstances. My life progressed right along at this point. I had no contact at all with any of my children and still do not to this day by their choosing. I have attempted to make contact but the authorities, child services and others have fought me on establishing any kind of contact with my youngest son, who is still a minor.

I received the following letter from child services regarding my youngest son. Upon receiving this letter it is apparent now as to his wishes. You have a 12 years old son who loves his dad. One day people walk into school and start asking him if he was molested by his dad. He does not even know what the word molested means.

His mother is telling him his dad did these horrible things to him and did them to his brother and sister. He has no memory of anything like this, because nothing ever happened to him and then you have some madman like Marion Knox telling him all of these things happened to him but he does not remember them happening because they were so horrible and terrible and he has forgotten them. UNBELIEVABLE!!!!

Then, the authorities believe it also. Oh come on, this can't be real. What a nightmare. All the while all he wants to know is "Dad are you going to come to my soccer game?" It breaks my heart, puts me in tears. I will never understand how responsible authorities can buy into all this stuff!

My two older children are adults so no restraining order was in place. The first restraining order kept me from contact with my youngest son until September of 2009. It lasted for one year. Looking back it's interesting about my youngest son. In chapter 2, I spoke of my last contact with my youngest son. It is amazing to me how he was telling me how much he loved me and just wanted me to come to his soccer game.

Now just 3 months later he did not want to see me or talk to me. He was afraid of me? He never had a chance. He was totally alienated from me based on false accusations. Susan Juster and the DHS were bound and determined to keep him from me no matter how much I did to prove my innocence. Looking back now, it was best these circumstances unfolded in the manner they did. In January of 2009, I received still another letter from the state of Oregon Child Services.

Received Time Jan. 29, 2009 2:07PM No. 2829

Linn County
Department of Health Services
P.O. Box 100, Albany, OR 97321

"Working together to promote the health and well-being of all Linn County residents"

1/29/09

Angie Janson,

This letter is in response to a request made by Zachary Skotko's Child Welfare case worker. I was asked to inform the court of any statements Zach had made to me regarding his wishes about contact with his father. Although initially hesitant to discuss events that had taken place in his family, Zach has since told me that he does not wish to live with his father. During a session on December 31st, 2008, Zach specifically stated that he does not wish to live with his father. He also stated that knowing the State has legal custody of him is a "relief," as he believes this will help protect him from his father. Although in a review of my progress notes I found I had not documented Zach's exact words, I do recall Zach indicating that he is scared of his father. During our sessions, Zach has not expressed a desire to have contact with his father.

If you wish to contact me, I can be reached at 967-3866 x 2337.

138

Well yes! He claims to have said he did not want to see me. All he heard for the past three months was how I had done all these things to him.

The state of Oregon determined I was a threat to my youngest son. Those allegations were based upon supposed testimony of my two older children who were saying they could not remember if I had actually done anything to them, but they believed those memories were repressed and only Mr. Marion Knox could help them discover them. So not only did the Police department originally believe Marion Knox, but basically the state did as well.

I draw those conclusions because both the police and state of Oregon included testimonies from Marion Knox and his wife and did not investigate them or check into any past history, which would include Marion Knox.

I am therefore apt to believe the authorities affirm these testimonies to be truthful and included them into their investigations. Now, I am going to show you a letter from the state Psychological board regarding Marion Knox. He was being investigated for practicing psychology. The following is a copy of the contents of the letter. The document is interesting as it led to some changes with the Evangelical Church

139

Alliance known as the ECA. The contents of the letter are as follows:

Oregon State Board of Psychological Examiners
3218 Pringle Rd. SE
Theodore Kulungoski, Governor
Salem, Oregon 97302
www.obpe.state.or.us

October 4, 2006
      Subject: Marion Knox, OPBE case #2005-060

Dear Mr. and Mrs. XXXXX

      The Board of Psychological Examiners has completed its review of the complaint you filed with this Board. The Board considered this matter at its meeting of September 29, 2006. After reviewing the facts, the Board concluded Mr. Knox's actions did not rise to the level of the "practice of psychology." The board does not have jurisdiction to issue orders against individuals whose "counseling" falls outside the definition, as follows:

The practice of psychology means rendering or offering to render supervision, consultation, evaluation, or therapy services to individuals, groups, or organizations for the purpose of diagnosing or treating behavioral, emotional or mental disorders (ORS 675.010 (4)).

The Board was of the opinion Mr. Knox's activities were not offered for the purpose of diagnosing or treating mental disorders. It voted to dismiss the complaint. This case is now closed. Nevertheless, Rev. Dr. Sam Goebel, President of the Evangelical Church Alliance (ECA), contacted me last week. As a result of a complaint made with the ECA against one of their Oregon licensures, the organization is developing a policy, which will not allow its licensures to perform exorcisms or other activities for the purpose of uncovering past "ritual abuse" in adult individuals. This is a positive development for affected families. I believe Dr. Loren Pankratz plans to speak with Dr. Goebel about developing this policy. Your complaint has been instrumental in this development. Thank you for coming forward.

Sincerely,
Karen Berry
OBPE Investigator

It appears the state of Oregon stepped in, to some degree, and helped put a stop to part of what was happening. Contacting the ECA effectively stripped a counselor by the name of Deborah Lacey of her ministerial credentials.

During my whole ordeal I never once had the opportunity to tell my side of the story. For a while this thought haunted me. With the traumatizing events of my life steadily speeding away and separating from me, I realize now this has been to my benefit.

Upon research it appears Marion Knox had aligned himself with other individuals. These individuals include Northwest Family Ministry's along with Clifford Baker and Deb Lacey. They worked together regularly in their therapy. Marion Knox spoke and ministered on occasion at the ministries conferences. I now deem this whole scenario as the "Mengele" pendulum.

Josef Rudolf Mengele was born 16 March 1911 and died 7 February 1979), he was also known as the Angel of Death (Todesengel in German). He was a German SS officer and a physician in the Nazi concentration camp Auschwitz-Birkenau. He earned doctorates in anthropology from Munich University and in medicine from Frankfurt University. He initially gained notoriety for being one of the SS physicians who supervised the selection of arriving transports of prisoners. He would determine who was to be killed and who was to become a laborer. He is far more infamous for performing grisly human experiments on camp inmates, for which Mengele was called the "Angel of Death".

In 1940, he was placed in the reserve medical corps, following he served with the 5th SS Panzergrenadier Division Wiking in the Eastern Front. In 1942, he was wounded at the Russian front and was pronounced medically unfit for combat, and was then promoted to the rank of SS-Hauptsturmführer (Captain) for saving the lives of three German soldiers. He survived the war, and after a period living incognito in Germany he fled to South America, where he evaded capture for the rest of his life despite being hunted as a Nazi war criminal.[1]

The "Mengele therapy" adopted by Knox, Lacey and the others, claims Joseph Mengele did not flee to South America, he did for a brief time before coming to The United States where he instructed the Masons and Satanic cults in the art of Sodomy. The theory claims when a child is between the ages of 2 and 4 the child's learning process is in between a fantasy and imaginative

143

states and a state where memories are more of a reality.

It is during this time Knox and the others claim if a child is sodomized he or she can be programmed and during this time the child is instilled with a demon, which will control its life.

Knox and the others claim they can exorcise this demon with their therapy. Knox claims this is in fact the cause for a large number of mental disorders including MPD, DID, and a host of physical ailments; these physical disorders include Cancer, Fibromyalgia, Arthritis, and the list goes on.

In May 1943, Mengele replaced another doctor who had fallen ill at the Nazi extermination camp Birkenau. On May 24, 1943, he became medical officer of Auschwitz-Birkenau "Gypsy camp". In August 1944, this camp was liquidated and all its inmates gassed. [2] Subsequently, Mengele became Chief Medical Officer of the main infirmary camp at Birkenau. He was not, though, the Chief Medical Officer of Auschwitz; superior to him was SS-Standortarzt (garrison physician) Eduard Wirths. [3]

During his 21-month stay at Auschwitz, Mengele earned the sobriquet "Angel of Death" for the cruelty he visited upon prisoners. Mengele was referred to as "der weiße Engel" ("the White

Angel") by camp inmates because when he stood on the platform inspecting new arrivals and directing some to the right, some to the left (the gas chambers), his white coat and white arms outstretched evoked the image of a white angel.

Mengele took turns with the other SS physicians at Auschwitz in meeting incoming prisoners at the camp, where it was determined who would be retained for work and who would be sent to the gas chambers immediately.[4] In one instance, he drew a line on the wall of the children's block 150 centimeters (about 5 feet) from the floor, and sent those whose heads could not reach the line to the gas chamber.[5] "He had a look, which said 'I am the power,'" said one survivor. When it was reported one housing block was infested with lice, Mengele ordered the 750 women assigned to and living there to be gassed. [6]

Notes Chapter 7:

[1] Stefan Kanfer and Peter Carls. "The Life and
       Crimes of a Nazi Doctor". People.
[2] http://en.auschwitz.org.pl
[3] "Eduard Wirths". Wsg-hist.uni-linz.ac.at.
       Retrieved 2010-12-28
[4] "Essay by Robert Jay Lifton". Wellesley.edu.
       1985-07-21. Retrieved 2010-03-01.
[5] Bülow, Louis. "Josef Mengele, Angel of
Death".   Retrieved 2008-12-16
[6] Mengele - The Final Account.
       [Documentary]. New York City, United
       States: History Channel. 2008-07-12.

Winter Forest by Edward McCabe

Chapter Eight
Digging for the truth

"If your therapist suggests you might have a repressed memory, check the small print on the wall plaque; he or she may be a correspondence-course therapist. Ditto for satanic abuse, which is so Eighties! Multiple personalities have been over-rated and past lives are now the preserve of Woman's Day." Deidre Macken (2004, April 23). Taken from "Off our trolley in the psychic marketplace," Australian Financial Times, page 44.

In the fall of 2006, the Evangelical Church Alliance headed by Dr. Sam Geobel, rescinded the credentials of counselor Debra Lacey after an investigation spurred by the previously mentioned families in Oregon. Lacey, who has a doctorate of divinity, called herself a "Soul Surgeon." She promoted herself as an expert on MPD.

In 2004, Lacey settled a lawsuit brought by Diane Lackey. Even though Lacey had settled the lawsuit with Lackey and her bizarre "therapy" had been exposed, Lacey continued to see clients. Parents of some of her other clients began to meet and soon nine people met with the Oregon Board of Psychologist Examiners to describe their concerns about two counselors; Lacey and a gospel singer by the name of Marion Knox of the Knox Brothers Gospel Quartet, who had been involved in devastating the families with their bizarre therapy and counseling.

The Oregon Psychological Examiners conducted a nine-month investigation but placed no sanctions against any of the counselors. Karen Berry, one of the Psychology Board Investigators told the families they needed to be in touch with the organization, which provided Lacey with her non-profit status and her minister's title since this is what protected her from the State's intervention.

The families contacted the Evangelical Church Alliance. They mailed much information to the Alliance. They sent family summaries, testimonials, and the attorney's summary from the former litigation. The families also told the church how they felt about counselors who hid behind a non-profit status. They said churches, which did nothing were actually harboring and sheltering harmful charlatans.

The church conducted its own investigation and quickly pulled Lacey's credentials. The ECA documented Deb Lacey failed to conduct herself according to the Pastoral Counselors Code of Ethics. Among these are the duties to:

-Evaluate the nature and potential causes of Ms. Lackey's problems;

-Engage in a "differential diagnosis." (Even though Ms. Lacey was not a licensed clinical psychologist, due care in the setting should include a consideration of all likely causes).

-Keep her adequately informed about available treatment;

-Provide the client with adequate warnings about any significant hazards or risks, which accompanied certain methodologies;

-Refrain from reinforcing methodologies and treatment which were known to be unscientific and lacked reliable independent corroboration.

The following is taken from the FMSF Newsletter 13 (3), May-June, 2004. Psychologist, Spiritual Counselor and "Soul Surgeon" Settle Case with former patient; Lackey v. Baker and Lacey. Case No. 0303-03121, filed Feb. 2001 Circuit Ct. Multnomah, County, OR.

After reading this report it became real apparent to me as to similarities with counsel my wife received from Marion Knox. I have in my possession a Training Manual from Northwest Family Ministries conference, which included sessions taught by Marion Knox. It is also my assumption upon failure in this case by Northwest Family Ministries, Knox transferred his recommended counseling to place blame upon a male figure as in the case of Mr. McCracken and me.

Knox changes his counseling approach from placing blame upon a "repressed memory" to placing blame on a male figure in the alleged victim's life. In the case of a solid family unit with average day to day struggles; this would indeed discredit the father and his role in the household and in raising and bringing discipline when warranted. Simply put, when ever discipline would be enforced in the home then the alleged victim would have to claim abuse, or assault and the police could bring arrest. This was the instance in my case.

Under Knox's influence this transpired over a period of 5 years in my home. Also, during this time my wife threatened on numerous occasions to flee, disappear, and forsake our marriage if I did not completely cooperate. It first started by us systematically severing relationship with friends. At certain times I needed to terminate certain employees, which became a threat to her. All of this was fueled by her physical ailments plaguing her. The situation then progressed to include family members. At first it was my wife's family starting with my stepson. Allegations arose in which he and his friends had abused the children when we were absent or when they were left with a baby sitter.

During this time I had a hotel remodeling business in Colorado Springs where we lived prior to Oregon. I traveled extensively with my business and when I was home we were together with the children. When I was home we never left the children alone with anybody. She did not trust anybody. In fact the reason we moved away from Colorado Springs is because she did not

151

trust anybody there. She had always been paranoid. Recently in 2010 I was able to speak with some old acquaintances and friends still residing in Colorado. They all hesitantly brought up the fact my wife was a very "private" person and really kept to herself. The accusations of sodomy then advanced to include her brother, then her father and Mother.

After this it systematically started to include my mother and father. Last, it landed on me. Over this time she would threaten to leave me and take the children. Claims were made by her, "there are places we could hide out, where we can never be found." At first light one would ask, how could you agree with all of this? When pressure like this builds over a 5-10 year period, things progress slowly and it is easy to conform to keep peace.

There were moments along the way of sanity when my wife was on medication for her ailments in which the allegations and threats would stop. Most of her medications were kept from me because she never told me she would go and seek medical attention. This added to the confusion on my part. This confusion was fueled by not knowing the circumstances as they were transpiring. The following is the report I spoke of in its entirety concerning the lawsuit against Deb

152

Lacey. I am including this report to show my circumstances are not an isolated event. This type of counseling is being performed by others. I also am including this report to bring validity to my situation.

[Psychologist, Spiritual Counselor and "Soul Surgeon"
Settle Case with Former Patient
Lackey v. DePaoli, Earl and NW Family Ministries,
Case No 0201-00733 filed Feb., 2002 and Lackey v. Baker and Lacey. Case No. 0303-03121, filed Feb. 2001 Circuit Ct. Multnomah County, Oregon. This report is written by Michael Shinn, Esq.
A final settlement of the extraordinary case of Diane Lackey v. Pastor Peter DePaoli and Rhonda Earle, dba [1] Northwest Family Ministries, Pastor Clifford A. Baker and Deborah Lacey, dba Catalyst Connections, Inc, defendants has been reached. This case shares similarities with many other false memory syndrome cases reported in the FMSF newsletter over the years. However, it features what may be a unique distinction: the therapists asserted Dr. Joseph Mengele, the notorious medical "experimenter" at Auschwitz, is the founder of Multiple

153

Personality Disorder in America, and he helped develop satanic rituals for the Masonic Temple, which Masons use to this day.

Diane Lackey is a dynamic, attractive mother and successful businesswoman. She also has a personal history, which included drug abuse and bisexual relationships. In June of 2001, she had a traumatic breakup with her life partner of three years. This sent her into a deep depression. She had a delusional episode in which she believed she was possessed by demons.

She began reading the Bible and rendering literal interpretations of it. She went to the New Song Church for "deliverance." There she met Pastor Cliff Baker who signed her up for his "prayer ministry" program. Participation in this program required her to sign a "legal release, assumption of the risk and indemnity agreement" which attempted to exonerate the pastor from all legal liability before his counseling had even begun. When she entered this program, Ms. Lackey had no memories whatsoever of being physically or sexually abused by anyone in her family. She had no memory of participating in any sex rituals as a child, or of being involved with Masons in any way.

During the ensuing four months, Diane dutifully attended Baker's sessions, which failed in any way to address what was later diagnosed as Bipolar Disorder. This manifested itself with delusions and hallucinations about demons and little inner voices. (Delusions are a key characteristic of several mental disorders). It never dawned on Pastor Baker these might be symptoms of a mental illness. Instead, he introduced Diane to Deb Lacey who has a doctorate in divinity. She has assigned herself the title of "Soul Surgeon" and promotes herself as an expert on MPD.

The "Soul Surgeon" worked with Diane Lackey in three lengthy sessions. Her "therapy" required Diane to describe and then to renounce every sexual act she had ever committed. She was compelled to do this in the presence of Lacey, Baker, and a "prayer intercessor." She found this humiliating and agonizing. Lacey did additional work with Diane's demons. Pastor Baker later testified he witnessed Diane levitating a foot above the floor and spinning around so furiously they had to pull her back into her chair to prevent her from hitting her head on the wall. (Lengthy sessions were a norm with Knox. Our first and seconds encounters lasted all day. This

<u>is when I stopped going and thought my family did also.)</u>

Ms. Lacey inquired about Diane's heritage. She wanted to know if anyone in her family had been a member of the Masons, Mormons, Odd fellows, Elks, Moose or Eagles lodges, Job's Daughters and the Rainbow or Order of Demolay. She elicited the fact an uncle had been a member of the Masons and declared therein lay the key to Diane's problems; presumably, membership in any of the other afore mentioned organizations would also have been inculpatory. She then required Diane to read a "Prayer of Release for Freemasons and Their Descendants" to Lacey, Baker, and the intercessor. This five page document included such passages as: "I renounce the oaths taken and the curses involved in the First or Entered Apprentice degree, especially their effects on the throat and tongue. I renounce the Hoodwink, the blindfold, and its effect on emotions and eyes, including all confusion, fear of the dark, fear of the light and fear of sudden noises.... I renounce the mixing and mingling of truth and error, and the blasphemy of this degree of Masonry. "When asked why Diane was forced to renounce Masonic activity of which she had no memory or known history whatsoever, Baker and Lacey

156

testified as a descendant of a Mason, she was equally afflicted and needed this cleansing ceremony. They overlooked the fact Diane was adopted and "Uncle Bob" was not even a blood relative.

(I would like to interject right here my wife was asked to pray the same prayer based on the fact she believed her father was a member in some sort of lodge, which was akin to Freemasonry).

Under the tutelage of Baker and Lacey, Diane began developing horrifying images of being subjected to lurid sex orgies with Uncle Bob and his Masonic colleagues. Deb Lacey persuaded Diane she had been victimized at the age of four, because this was the age she assigned to one of her inner voices, Sarah. Diane confronted Uncle Bob about these activities, and promised to expose him. He wisely reported this to the local police and to her father. Her father informed her by "e-mail" Uncle Bob didn't even join the Masons until she was 13 and there was no indication she was ever abused by anyone as an infant or child. By now, Diane believed she was possessed by eleven alter personalities. Perplexed by her father's e-mail, she inquired of Pastor Baker if these might be false memories.

No, he said, lying about their guilt was characteristic of Masons. She needed to trust her new memories and could expect to retrieve more of them.

(Again here; this was the same counsel Marion Knox gave my wife. Masons were liars and to trust her new memories as being the bona fide truth).

To assist her in this adventure, Baker brought her to Pastor Peter DePaoli (a licensed clinical psychologist) at Northwest Family Ministries. During her first session there, Diane was shown a videotape of Dr. Joseph Mengele and the Auschwitz death camp. Questioned about this in depositions, DePaoli claimed he knew little about Mengele and just happened to show her the video because she had some questions about Mengele. I impeached DePaoli with a 45-minute tape recording of a speech he gave in 1998 in which he told the International Conference of Pastoral Counselors his research had uncovered the fact Mengele was the "father of MPD in America," (where he came after WWII and not to Argentina). DePaoli convinced Diane Lackey she was possessed by a Mengele demon, among many others.

(Same counsel again, Early on in our whole involvement with Marion Knox I knew this was "bunk". I remember being in high school in 1979 when we heard of Joseph Mengele dying. We had discussion on it. To my knowledge and learning Mengele never came to the United States. There is documented proof He spent his entire post World War II life in South America.)

Throughout the course of the summer of 2002, Diane was plagued with terrifying images of Joseph Mengele, Masonic temple orgies, blood sacrifices, and demons of all varieties.
(Marion Knox had my wife believing she had been involved in a satanic ritual through her father's lodge wherein she was supposedly involved with a human infant sacrifice. During this ritual he led her to believe she had drunk the blood of a human infant sacrifice. This is the same line of questioning we reported early, in which he had taken others through; the drinking of a human infant's blood being sacrificed.)

When these images became so bizarre she realized they were not likely true, she informed Baker she suspected they were false memories. She was considering suing DePaoli. In response, Baker affirmed DePaoli's work and promptly terminated his counseling relationship with her.

(This was the same time frame Mr. McCracken was being investigated in Brownsville Oregon,

159

based on the allegations of a young female. Brownsville is located very close to Albany. Those charges were dropped by the Lynn County District Attorney's office at the last minute, when it was reported the accuser had sought counsel with Marion Knox. The "demon" named by the accuser in this instance was named "Joseph" as in Joseph Mengele. Prior to such counseling by Marion Knox it is reported the girl was in a deep state of lethargy and unresponsive to any treatment at the hospital. The family denied the girl was ever abused but Knox insisted she indeed had been).

When she came to my law office, I referred her to competent mental health professionals. After months of therapy and psychiatric medication, she finally broke away from the demon delusions and was able to revive her nearly bankrupt business. Early in the legal proceedings, Pastor Baker filed a motion to have the case dismissed noting he was a "spiritual" counselor and his First Amendment rights protected him. The plaintiff argued a counselor was like a primary care physician, with the responsibility not only to treat problems, but also to recognize and diagnose problems, which are beyond the counselor's ability to treat. Although

160

he was her pastor, he was also her professional counselor and provided direct therapeutic services and arranged for additional psychological care from others. As such, he was bound by the responsibilities detailed in the Pastoral Counselors' Code of Ethics. Among these were the duties to:

Evaluate the nature and potential causes of her problems;

Engage in a "differential diagnosis." (Even though he was not a licensed clinical psychologist, due care in the setting should include a consideration of all potential causes rather than limited ones.);

Keep him adequately informed about available treatment;

Provide the client with adequate warnings about any significant hazards or risk accompanied certain methodologies;

Refrain from reinforcing methodologies and treatment which were known to be unscientific and lacked reliable independent corroboration. Plaintiff's attorney: Michael R. Shinn of Portland, Portland, Oregon.

Defendants' attorneys: Michael Hoffman, Paul Cooney, David Ryan of

Portland, Oregon. [1] "dba" refers to "doing business as."]

"It is not enough to demand evidence and answers from accusers. It is necessary to extend justice to those who are and have been wrongfully accused."
End of Michael Shinn's report.

No one may ever know the amount of lonely people who were in need of a friend and sought out these mentioned for counsel. Numbers of people have had their lives further torn apart by trusting in these who claim this type of counseling. There are a lot of individuals who conduct outlandish "deliverance" type of ministries who are no better equipped to diagnose people's conditions than the next individual. They may truly believe they are helping people and their motives might be good, but stricter legislation needs to be put into place to guard against these fallacies continuing. Good people are being hurt and some are facing prison times because they simply sought help from someone they trusted.

Chapter Nine
A bit of history

"It is what it is," and "Things aren't always what they seem to be." Unknown

Marion Knox, Deb Lacey, NW Family Ministries and Baker are the individuals who base their therapy on the results of medical experiments conducted by Joseph Mengele, the "Angel of Death." They claim Mengele never went to South America after World War II, but

163

indeed came to The United States and brought his teachings to the order of the Freemasons through Aleister Crowley. These individuals claim to be Christians and invoke the true teachings of Jesus Christ in order to experience superiority over others.

Their line of therapy and counseling in my opinion is nothing short of wanting to gain control and power over others suffering from a host of ailments. Again I constantly ask myself and have made the statement early in this book; why would these people, this man Marion Knox want to push this form of therapy. We have proof it damages homes, ruins the lives of individuals, businesses, and creates havoc in communities and churches.

Already documented in this book from reliable sources are stories of teachers, business people and hard working individuals who have suffered great loss, endured public and private humiliation, and yet; some of these so called therapists and counselors continue to practice their therapy. In my instance it falls prey on an average family with normal and acceptable problems, which were magnified into being felony charges, which could have resulted in extensive prison sentences.

I think it is appropriate at this time to bring to light who Aleister Crowley and Joseph Mengele really were. I am in no way condoning any of Crowley's teachings or to the actions of Mengele. In my early adulthood I was a self seeking history individual of World War II. I have and had numerous uncles who fought in World War II. Probably, one half of the readers of this book will have known someone or were acquainted with someone who sacrificed their time and young adulthood fighting either Hitler's Germany or Japan.

I am truly appalled at what transpired and what was permitted to transpire during this particular portion of world history. It was an era of history where I look back and am ashamed to read about what transpired and what was permitted to transpire as with the Tuskegee experiments.

I have personally visited Poland and Western Russia on a number of occasions in the early 1990's. I have visited Auschwitz. I walked the grounds of the camp. I visited the prisoner barracks. I placed my head into the ovens, which were used by Joseph Mengele to exterminate thousands of people. Present to this day are protein remains of human bodies plastered on the walls inside those ovens. Those ovens became the final resting place of thousands of well respected people at one point of their life. I toured a former concentration camp in Northern Poland where the piles of human hair, piles of the shoe soles, and mounds of eyeglasses frames have been left as a memorial to those who perished in those death camps.

Since my story surrounds the counseling and therapy of Marion Knox and this counseling surrounds and bases itself on the myth of these men contributing to the spread and development of Multiple Personality Disorder and Dissociative Identity Disorder (referred to as MPD and DID); I deem this chapter important for others to fully understand the consequences I was forced to deal with and endure. Diane Lackey was forced the humiliation of this sort of therapy. I am thankful she received the help she needed.

It is widely believed Crowley was not a true Freemason as Knox and these others claim he was. Crowley claims the following; 33° of the Scottish rite in Mexico from Don Jesus Medina. The United Grand Lodge of England, whose recognition is generally considered the standard for Masonic validity, did not recognize any of the above bodies as being true Freemasonry, thus Crowley never was an "official" Freemason within the common understanding of the term. It is unlikely the Claims of Baker and DePaoli are valid as the involvement of Crowley and Mengele with Freemasonry. It is also very unlikely the two men ever met with Crowley's death coming in 1947 in England. He had been ill for a number of years. [7]

Mengele's experiments were gruesome and grisly and he experimented with the effects of heredity and other human trial and error experiments. Mengele used Auschwitz as an opportunity to continue his research on heredity, using inmates for human experimentation. He was particularly interested in identical twins; they would be selected and placed in special barracks.

He also recruited Berthold Epstein, a Jewish pediatrician. As a doctor, Epstein proposed to Mengele a study into treatments of the disease called Noma, which was noted for particularly affecting children from the camp. [1] While the exact cause of Noma remains uncertain, it is now known it has a higher occurrence in children suffering from malnutrition and a lower immune system response. Many develop the disease shortly after contracting another illness such as measles or tuberculosis. [2]

Mengele took an interest in physical abnormalities discovered among the arrivals at the concentration camp. These included dwarfs, notably the Ovitz family - the children of a Romanian artist, of whom seven of the ten members were dwarfs.

Prior to their deportation, they toured in Eastern Europe as the Lilliput Troupe. Mengele often called them "my dwarf family"; to him they seemed to be the perfect expression of "the abnorm".[3] Mengele's experiments also included attempts to take one twin's eyeballs and attach them to the back of the other twin's head, changing eye color by injecting chemicals into children's eyes, various amputations of limbs, and other surgeries.

Rena Gelissen's account of her time in Auschwitz details certain experiments performed on female prisoners around October 1943. Mengele would experiment on the chosen girls performing sterilization and shock treatments. Most of the victims died, because of either the experiments or later infections.

Mengele's assistant once rounded up 14 pairs of Roma twins during the night. Mengele placed them on his polished marble dissection table and put them to sleep. He then injected chloroform into their hearts, killing them instantly. Mengele then began dissecting and meticulously noting each piece of the twins' bodies." [3]

At Auschwitz, Mengele did a number of twin studies. After the experiment was over, these twins were usually killed and their bodies dissected. He supervised an operation by which two Romani children were sewn together to create conjoined twins; the hands of the children became badly infected where the veins had been resected, this also caused gangrene. [3]

The subjects of Mengele's research were better fed and housed than ordinary prisoners and were, for the time being, safe from the gas chambers, although many experiments result in more painful deaths.[4] When visiting his child subjects, he introduced himself as "Uncle Mengele" and offered them sweets. Some survivors remember despite his grim acts, he was also called "Mengele the protector". [5]

The book "Children of the Flames", by Lucette Matalon Lagnado and Shiela Cohn Dekel, chronicles Mengele's medical experimental activities on approximately 3,000 twins who passed through the Auschwitz death camp during World War II until its liberation at the end of the war. Only 100 pairs of twins survived.[5] 60 years later, they came forward about the special privileges they were given in

Auschwitz owing to Mengele's interest in twins, and how as a result they have suffered, as the children who survived his medical experiments and injections. [3]

Auschwitz prisoner Alex Dekel has said: "I have never accepted the fact Mengele himself believed he was doing serious work — not from the slipshod way he went about it. He was only exercising his power. Mengele ran a butcher shop — major surgeries were performed without anesthesia. Once, I witnessed a stomach operation — Mengele was removing pieces from the stomach, but without any anesthetic. Another time, it was a heart, which was removed, again without anesthesia. It was horrifying.

Mengele was a doctor who became mad because of the power he was given. Nobody ever questioned him — why did this one die? Why did this one perish? The patients did not count. He professed to do what he did in the name of science, but it was madness on his part." [6]

I felt it appropriate to include this brief history of Josef Mengele, the man who these therapists claim is the cause for so much pain and suffering. They claim his experiments and his fascination with "Sodomy" and as Knox describes "Mengele's perfect art of sodomizing a child." It is their assessment these two men's obsession with sodomy and satanic ritual abuse at the hands of the Masons and every satanic cult is the sole cause of MPD, DID, and a host of Physical ailments.

Upon further examination one wonders who is causing the most destruction to people. How many individuals have been falsely accused? How many children are separated from their mothers and fathers because of this therapy I call "madness." I truly believe they teach and use this therapy in a twisted way to possess some sort of control to over those who are honestly seeking help. I really want to challenge anyone who claims to have benefited from the therapy of Marion Knox and these others to come forward and share a testimony. One such website; www.ritualabusefree.com has a testimony of one woman named "Jane." As of January 1, 2011 their website posts the following "testimony":

Jane: My Celebration of Deliverance

Family of Origin:

I came from a multi-generational high-level bloodline occult family. I was purposely conceived and birthed for mind control, torture and ritual purposes. My family's background includes high level Masonic members and connections. I have three half-sisters and one half-brother. My mother and surrogate father were extreme alcoholics. Chaos was the norm. I was singled out as the scapegoat for abuse by all members of the family. I continually experienced every type of abuse imaginable, including physical, gross sexual, rape, sodomy, extreme neglect, poverty, and forced child pornography, and prostitution.

We moved very frequently. During my seventeen years at home, we lived in twenty-seven different houses in four states. I attended twelve different schools using alias names in each new locale. I was extremely isolated by my parents. I did not know everyone didn't wake up and look in the mirror and find they were two years older and living in a different house and going to a different school. I thought terror, starvation, torture, and abuse were normal.

I was born with a cleft pallet and harelip, and was in continuous ill health during my growing years. Medical care was given only when I was in a life-threatening situation. Otherwise it was a luxury.

Escape and Hope:

172

My first husband was handpicked by my parents and I was forced to marry at seventeen years of age. Abuse and control continued. This marriage did give me the opportunity to move to California and put some distance away from the horror of my family. I had two daughters; I was divorced after four years. With my second husband Ted I found myself truly loved and cherished for the first time in my life. He loved and raised my children as if they were his own. We've been married 25 years.

In February 1977 I accepted Jesus Christ as my personal Lord and Savior by reading Corrie Ten Boom's book "The Hiding Place." As Corrie knew Jesus amidst the horror of the concentration camps, I recognized Jesus had been with me in the midst of the horror of my childhood, continuously drawing me and wooing me. Now as His child I found a measure of hope and security and a knowing of His love, which enabled me to trust and find courage to face all, which was coming. As an adult I always likened my life to being born in a concentration camp. Only God in His matchless wisdom would use Corrie's story of a concentration camp to reach me and save me.

Falling Apart at the Seams:

Once I was secure in my second marriage, my tenuous health fell to pieces. The childhood abuse now needed attention. The ensuing years brought twenty-one major surgeries of reconstruction and repair due to the earlier abuse and torture. I was on a medical merry-go-round with hemorrhages, immune disorders, unexplained skin disorders, a wide range of gastric disorders, chronic pain, infections, major dental and oral problems, and extreme anemia. This resulted in numerous hospitalizations apart from the surgeries. I saw an endless array of medical specialists and was treated numerous times at Stanford Hospital.

I did not enter into serious psychotherapy until my surrogate father died. Following his death, flashbacks and memories began flooding and I commenced the long, arduous journey of nineteen years of intense psychotherapy and thirteen years under the watch of a psychiatrist. The professionals were often at a loss as to understand what had happened to me and how best to help me. One therapist and author was able to use my story when lecturing to students at

Harvard Medical School about recognizing the signs of abuse in their future patients. It was very difficult to work with me at times for sure. I am grateful for the ones who hung with me throughout the journey. I have been told case histories like mine usually require institutionalization and rarely attain normal functioning. However, throughout it all I was somewhat functional, which gave me some hope.

After 13 years of therapy I did seem to level off and took a break from the regimen. But soon there was more. I began working with a Christian therapist, who specialized in Dissociative Identity Disorder and Ritual Abuse. He also taught college graduate studies in the field of DID. Over the next 51/2 years 340 alter personalities were identified, and multitudes of layered fragments were found in my multiple system. Some integration occurred, and then my situation became nightmarishly worse.

My physical health plummeted. I was diagnosed with Critical Lung Disease, and Critical Asthma. Painful cracked ribs were the norm resulting from severe coughing bouts. Pneumonia onsets were frequent. Fibromyalgia like pains were debilitating. Fatigue was constantly with me. My immune system became nearly non-functional. Serious anemia required

175

ongoing monitoring. I no longer responded to IV antibiotics. I was blessed by being under the watchful care of more medical specialists, but their best efforts were not bringing improvement to my condition. I was actually getting worse. My therapist then began to do deliverance sessions, which helped to a degree. However, I began to really sense my struggle was much bigger in the spiritual dimension then he or I was aware of. It felt like my physical and emotional life was draining away. I was increasingly consumed with terror day and night. I was rarely sleeping and when I did the night terrors were hideous beyond description.

Answered Prayer & Deliverance:

In December of 1998 I began to pray to God and asked He would send someone who could truly help me; I knew who ever it would be was going to have to be more knowledgeable in spiritual warfare and deliverance than anyone I was aware of out there in the Christian realm. In March 1999 my therapist was invited to observe Marion Knox work with victims of extreme ritual abuse. He went as a clinical observer not with my case in mind at all. As Marion was working my therapist realized they were describing some detailed rituals and mutilation, which I had

176

uncovered in my therapy. He asked me to talk to Marion. When I did, Marion asked questions for which I had answers all my life. Up to this point, no medical or psychological professional or pastor had ever asked me the questions.

On May 3, 1999 with my husband and therapist participating, by God's grace Marion, in a three hour telephone conference call, delivered me of my Legion & DID system. I had immediate and complete integration. I was whole in my mind for the first time ever. God did in three hours, what I had attempted to do in over 19 years of therapy at a cost of nearly $180,000!!!

Once the confusion and fragmentation of my mind was healed and not able to serve as the "smoke and mirrors" for my demonic system to hide behind, all hell broke loose in more physical and mental fury. My ritual programming and infirmities seemed to implode. By mid August 1999 there was nothing more, which could be done for me medically or psychologically. I believed I was dying.

My husband and I traveled to Marion's home in late October 1999. Over a span of twenty-seven hours, Marion found the strongman, Josef, of my demonic system and removed him and the deep programming which resided within me. My infirmity systems departed as well. On November 2, 1999, I was physically, spiritually and emotionally healed. I had immediate indications my asthma and fibromyalgia were gone. At the time I got to Oregon I was taking over fifteen medications and several inhalers plus using a Nebulizer to assist breathing every two hours around the clock. I now take one routine prescription medication and am otherwise medication free for the first time in my life. At one point I was taking several psychotropic medications, which I was told I would need for the rest of my life due to chemical imbalances in my brain. I am now pain free, and there continues to be no trace of asthma or lung disease. Even lung scarring which appeared in x-rays has disappeared. On returning from Oregon I stopped therapy and gradually was released by my key doctors.

Today I enjoy a clean bill of health. Spiritually, I have a passion for the Lord along with awesome joy and peace. I feel like I am in an envelope of peace! I no longer have fear after walking, talking and breathing terror for 47 years. God's Word is vibrant and the struggle to grow and move forward in my Christian walk is gone! I am truly able to love the Lord with all my heart, all my mind and all my soul and strength!!! I can truly say with Christ all things are possible!

All the kings' horses and all the kings' men could not put me together and render me whole. Only the King of King's Himself could do it.

Psalm 86: 11-13 (Amplified Version) Teach me Your way, O Lord, may I may and live in Your truth; direct and unite my heart (solely, reverently) to fear and honor Your name. I will confess and praise You, O Lord my God, with my whole (united) heart; and I will glorify your name forevermore. For great is your mercy and loving-kindness toward me; and you have delivered me from the depths of Sheol (from exceeding depths of affliction).

Jane
crosstofreedom@aol.com

Upon discovering this post Gale Millard and I sent an email to this address. It was returned to us. We then contacted this website and asked for further information and they stated "they no longer have contact with 'Jane,' and have not had contact with her in quite some time." When we asked them this question here was there response:

From: "ritualabusefree@cs.com"
<ritualabusefree@cs.com>
To: twokayaks@yahoo.com
Sent: Sun, December 26, 2010 4:42:00 AM
Subject: Re: Freedom
Hello,
I am sorry, but I have lost contact with Jane. The e-mail address does not work. I have had some computer crashes and lost some address data as well. I have heard from others who have been healed and yes, it takes time and a lot of courage. With God's help, you can be set free. I might suggest you get a copy of our healing workbook, From Victims to Victors, as it has helped many people. We usually use it when doing personal ministry as well as leading from the Holy Spirit. You can work through it by yourself or with a trusted friend or pastor.

It does not use any methods of memory retrieval, but sometimes it does bring back some memories when you deal with each topic. You can find a table of contents and a portion of the book on our Book page if you click on the link by the book title.

I often help people work through the book by phone after they get a copy. I understand some of your pain as I, too, am a survivor. I wrote a

180

good portion of the book and if you have read the Poems on the poem page on our web site, I am the author of them as well.

Blessings, Donna
www.ritualabusefree.org

Upon questioning the "ministers" at ritualabusefree.org through emails, we received a response from "Sister Donna" stating "they did not have anything to do with Marion Knox or his form of ministry and therapy" Here is the email we received with our original question:
From: "fojcministries@cs.com"
<fojcministries@cs.com>
To: helpforvictims@yahoo.com
Sent: Sun, December 19, 2010 6:30:40 AM
Subject: Re: Marion Knox and his deceptive therapy practices
No, we are not affiliated with Marion Knox, nor do we follow any of his practices. We are not affiliated with any denomination or organization. We offer healing through what Jesus did on the cross. We have had experience in casting out demons and also working with MPD/DID. However, we believe it is a process, but all in God's timing.
+

Feel free to ask any more questions.
 Blessings, Sister Donna
www.ritualabusefree.org

-----Original Message-----
From: Teila Tankersley
<helpforvictims@yahoo.com>
To: FOJCMinistries@cs.com
Sent: Sat, Dec 18, 2010 11:22 pm
Subject: Marion Knox and his deceptive therapy
practices
Please tell me you are not affiliated with Marion
Knox?

I am afraid I am having trouble believing
in Marion Knox's tactics, I have a hard time
understanding how his out dated and abusive
therapy is condone in the Christian community? I
have read his interviews and have interviewed
several of his former patients and I believe he is
destroying families and is leading his vulnerable
clients into believing they have been
sodomized. I stumbled upon your site and am
surprised you are supporting his beliefs; please
tell me it isn't so.

Respectfully,
Teila Tankersley

Now this all strikes me very funny. Why does this website still list this testimony on their website? If it is such a powerful testimony for them why would they let their communication and contact fall to the wayside concerning "Jane"? One would think someone this important for them to list this testimony would be available for comment. Then the question arises; if they do not condone the practices, therapy and counseling of Marion Knox, why do they even list this testimony. Maybe they get book sales because of it! It is clear; they suggested we buy their book as a result of "Jane's" testimony.

This is all very interesting to me. So "Jane" who are you and where are you? Please step forward and talk to me. Make yourself known. You have had such a powerful experience at the hands of Marion Knox and we would like to interview you.. I really want to believe you were healed and "delivered" through this form of counseling. I am sure with all of your ailments there is documented medical charts, notes, and other statements from physicians who can validate your claims.

Ritual abuse free and other websites like them are all over the internet. Another interesting note is they claim they are not affiliated with any denomination or organization. This is very interesting. This decision on their part comes with no oversight into their therapy practices. They are free to develop outlandish bogus therapy based on their own personal beliefs as have Depaoli, Baker, Lacey and Knox. I also failed to see any testimonies listed there of individuals they have helped with their "Healing workbook". By her own admission "she is also a survivor".

Notes Chapter 8:

[1] "Page 296-297". Holocaust-history.org. 07-23-2005. Retrieved 12-01-2010

[2] "German article at". Shoa.de. Retrieved 12-01-2010

[3] Bülow, Louis. "Josef Mengele, Angel of Death". Retrieved 12-1-2010

[4] Lagnado, Lucette Matalon; Sheila Cohn Dekel (1991). Children of the Flames.ISBN 0688096956.

[5] "Josef Mengele and Experimentation on Human Twins at Auschwitz". Longwood.k12.ny.us. Retrieved 12-01-2010

[6] Dr. Josef Mengele, ruthless Nazi concentration camp doctor - The Crime Library on truTV.com". Crimelibrary.com. Retrieved 12-01-2010

[7] E.g. Starr M P 2004, "Alistair Crowley: freemason!"\ Grand Lodge of British Columbia and Yukon, http://freemasonry.bcy.ca/aqc/crowley.html

Mystical Window Anonymous photographer

Chapter Ten
The Investigation Continues

"Once you eliminate the impossible, whatever remains, no matter how improbable, must be the truth." Sir Arthur Conan Doyle

What can a man do when the person he loves with his whole heart is promising she is not

186

receiving counseling from such a man as Marion Knox, but is without his knowledge? Over the five years my wife was seeking his counsel, I would beg her to leave Oregon on numerous occasions.

"Let's move away" I'd say, "We can start over." "Let's move closer to family so the children can have a relationship with their grandmother, aunts, uncles, and cousins."

She would refuse because of course Knox had her believing our families abused my children as well. I mean Knox had her and my children believing everyone had abused them. I mean "My gosh man! When does the insanity of it all stop." I would think to myself.

When does the law step in and stop individuals like Knox from hiding behind a cloak of clergy. As I am writing the words of this particular chapter, I am being inundated with "emails" from individuals stepping up with all sorts of stories of their ordeals with Knox.

On January 2, 2011, The Albany, Oregon, Democrat Herald ran a front-page story of my impending lawsuit against Knox. The newspaper there in Oregon was alerted to my legal actions when another family affected by Knox saw the first Internet article written and posted by Teila Tankersley. Within a few days a reporter was

187

emailing me wanting to write this piece for their paper.

This one act has opened the hearts of many individuals who have been drug through the mud as I have. Most of these people have had their homes restored to some sort of peace, but the damage lingers on. Most are glad to have been reunited with their children, parents, brothers and sisters. To come out now and speak again of the atrocities and heartache they have suffered is difficult. It opens the "Can of worms again" Some of the relationships are fragile at best and others have solidified and returned to semi-normalcy. But, all feel some amount of effects of this counseling.

It is an interesting note as I write these words; Knox counsels all these people the same They had events, which have traumatized them as a child so much they can't remember them. He then watches as the homes are torn apart and goes about his life as a farmer in his nice tractor, plowing his fields. He travels with his brothers and sings gospel songs, has cruises where supporters can travel with their gospel quartet, and is part owner of a construction company with his sons.

All these families came to Knox to really get help, then he watches them go through the gut wrenching effects of this counseling. In the end when it's all over they will forever have memories of their traumatizing ordeal with Knox. Interesting is they never forget these memories. The memories of his counseling never get repressed!

There are hundreds if not thousands of people in Oregon affected by Knox' quest for power and control. By just conducting an internet search; one discovers a whole host of "Ministries" with claims of "Deliverance, Deprogramming, and Restoration" of your soul. Like we stated earlier we found one with a long entailed "testimony" to Knox' counseling who claim they have nothing to do with him. Most of them are Pentecostal by nature, but there are others.

In the newspaper article by the Albany Democrat Herald it talks about church based counselors being exempt. The problem with Marion and Doris Knox is they hold no official credentials or any sort of ministerial licenses. How do you govern counselors like them? In the article they list the following:

"New license guidelines for professional therapists": New state licensing requirements for professional counselors and marriage and family therapists took effect with the start of the New

*Year, but church-based counselors such as
Marion and Doris Knox are not affected by the
new rules. Current laws provide some
exemptions from licensing requirements for
counselors and therapists, Beck Eklund,
executive director of the Oregon Board of
Licensed Professional Counselors and
Therapists, explained in a statement from Salem.
"This change will require counselors and
therapists in private practice — those who
diagnose and treat clients for mental health
disorders — need to be licensed." Recognized
members of the clergy may provide counseling
without a license. So may professional
counselors and marriage and family therapists in
public agencies. Such agencies include schools
and city, county, state or federal agencies,
Eklund said.*

*Licensed professional counselors and licensed
marriage and family therapists must meet the
following requirements:*

    *• Earn at least a master's degree from an
accredited university.*

    *• Pass a national competency exam and a
state exam about laws and administrative rules,
which govern the profession.*

    • Abide by a code of ethics.

• Complete ongoing education in the mental health field.

• Respond to complaints submitted to the state licensing board.

Counseling clients should ask questions of their potential counselors or therapists and check the state licensing board's website to find out if counselors or therapists have licenses. Clients can also find out whether a counselor has violated laws or rules. The website of the Oregon Board of Licensed Professional Counselors and Therapists is at www.oregon.gov/oblpct.

It may appear now I could have stopped it all. People have said over and over to me, "Why didn't you just stop them from going to visit Knox?" Well, I did not know to what extent they were going to see him and exactly how much they saw of him. I did at times tell my wife, "Do not take my children there", and for a while they did not go to visit Knox.

I was the sole bread winner in the family. My wife did not work a job until just a few years before the nightmare began. Some of my work days were long as required because of being self employed. Most of these visits transpired during the day when I was gone. I was to discover at a

191

later date my wife went to see a social worker in May of 2008, four months prior to my arrest, without my knowledge. They instructed her to wait for a later date to call the police and file a formal complaint.

During those four months our home continued to function normally as it had all along. There were periods over the last five years we were together in peace and then there were periods of total confusion and chaos. There were no quarrels except concerning Knox's involvement in our home, and we continued to be intimately involved with each other. In fact this was never an issue in our marriage. In the Police report my wife claims I confessed to her and the Knox's I indeed did sexually molest all of my children. In the DHS hearing in April of 2009, both of the Knox's testified under oath I had not said such a thing. So who do you believe?

The original police "investigation" (a very loose term in my books) had detective Fairall and Dawn Hietala interviewing and questioning Marion and Doris Knox. Detective Fairal interviewed Marion and Detective Hietala interviewed Doris Knox. I have included the supplemental report. In it Doris Knox states my relationship with my wife was "abusive" Then she states my wife never complained of any abuse taking place. So why would she say it was abusive if no accusations were made? How would Doris Knox draw such a conclusion?

Doris Knox then claims my wife caught her father sodomizing my youngest son. Supposedly my son slept through the whole event. This was to have taken place while my wife and children were visiting them in Indiana the previous summer. I have never been able to figure out how this event suddenly transpired in my son's life. I also do not believe an 80+ year-old man can anally sodomize a 12 year old boy while my son was sleeping and my son not waking up during such an event?

I am sorry, I do not believe it and I do not accept it, short of the fact the Knox's had all to do with this outlandish story! Another point here is Doris Knox states my children had no memory of any sexual abuse-taking place at my hands except they had a "feeling" something had. Doris Knox further states this "feeling" only came over my children when Marion Knox prayed for them.

This interview was conducted on 9-18-2008 and the supplemental report written by Detective Hietala on 9-19-2008. The main police report was written by Detective Fairall on 9-22-2008. It was actually written later because Detective Fairall would interview my daughter

193

on 9-21-2008.

In the interview my daughter goes on for 2 pages with accusations about me, which supposedly transpired in her life over the previous 8 years; all sorts of stories of abuse, sodomy and assault which was to have happened on a daily basis. So as far as my daughter is concerned nothing ever happened with no memories until Marion prayed for her; then in the police report stating eight years of abuse on a nightly basis! This is hard to accept and I cannot but think somehow Knox planted these thoughts. Here is the supplemental report.

SUPPLEMENTAL REPORT

Incident #:	Date/Time of Original Report:	Date/Time of this report:
08-20100	09/18/2008 @ 0904hrs.	09/19/2008 @ 2244hrs.

SUSPECT(S):

Skotko, Steve

SUMMARY:

On 09-18-08 I spoke with Doris Knox at her residence located at 36185 Bolhken Drive, Lebanon, Linn County, Oregon. I spoke to Doris about her knowledge of incidents that may have occurred in the Skotko family.

ACTION TAKEN:

On 09-18-08 at about 1400 hours Detective G. Fairall asked me to assist him by accompanying him out to the Knox residence and interviewing Doris Knox while he separately interviewed her husband Marion Knox.

Upon arrival at 36185 Bolhken Drive, the Knox residence, Detective Fairall introduced us and asked if the Knox's would be willing to speak with us. Both Marion and Doris Knox said they would. Detective Fairall went with Marion Knox into a separate part of the house and I spoke with Doris in the kitchen.

I advised Doris that our conversation was being recorded and she acknowledged the recorder. I told Doris that Peggy Skotko had come to the Albany Police Department and made a report. I asked Doris if she knew something about what Peggy might have reported. I did not tell Doris what the report regarded.

Doris told me that she believes she and Marion Knox met Peggy about two years ago. Doris said that Peggy contacted them so because she had heard that Marion could help people. Doris told me that people just call Marion for counseling and prayer. Doris told me Marion is not a licensed counselor he just helps people. Doris was not specific in how Peggy had heard about Marion but that may have been because she really did not know.

Doris told me that Peggy relationship with Steve Skotko had been abusive but she did not specifically recall Peggy complaining about physical abuse. Doris said there had been issues with the children acting out and that was one of the reasons Peggy wanted to talk with Marion.

Doris said Peggy reported to them that she had caught her father sexually abusing her youngest son. Then Doris went on to tell me the story of the incident. Doris said Peggy was visiting her family out of state. She said Peggy got up in the middle of the night and Peggy observed her father coming from the room Peggy's youngest son was sleeping in. Doris told me Peggy reported her father was not wearing any pants. Peggy reportedly then went into her son's room and found him "to be a mess." Doris told me she is uncertain if the son remembers this because he was asleep when it occurred. Doris reports that the grandfather anally sodomized the boy. Doris also told me that it did not occur to Peggy until after she left her father's house that anal sodomy had occurred, but she realized that was the only thing that could have happened to cause her son to be "in a mess" like that.

Doris talked about the other children, an older boy and an older sister, Keri, "having a feeling" that anal sodomy may have occurred to them also with the perpetrator being their own father, Steve Skotko. Doris told me neither the older son nor the older daughter had concrete memory of it occurring rather they just had a "feeling." Doris told me the feeling came over them when her husband Marion was doing "deliverance" on them.

I asked Doris to tell me what "deliverance" was. Doris explained that was when Marion spoke to the

Reporting Officer	DPSST#	Shift:	Assignment:	Supervisor Approval:
Dawn Hietala	24086	Detectives.		

Suspect Supplemental Report

Knox believes the majority of individuals living today has been either sodomized or has suffered some sort of sexual abuse.

I want to pose a question to you the reader at this time. According to Marion Knox up words of 90% of the population of the world has been either sodomized or suffered abuse at the hands of some satanic ritual ceremony. If this were to be true, there is a 90% chance you the reader have been sodomized at some point in your life.

Knox, Baker, DePaoli, and Lacey all claim if your family includes someone in the Masons, had Catholicism or Mormonism as your religion, or were a member of some other fraternal order; you were sodomized as a child. This was the case of the Brownsville, Oregon man and this was the case with Diane Lackey.

Stop and think, do you have a memory of such an event happening in your life? To get down to earth this means a male placed his sex organ in your Anus! Did this happen to you? This might sound crude to you, but this was the exact question they posed to me during my polygraph test. Marion Knox would assert it did happen, but you don't remember because it's so horrific you would forget it because it's to traumatizing. Better yet, you would not remember it because

196

you were being programmed like a robot so at a later date you would have your "triggering mechanism pulled" and you would do something or commit an act of terrorism.

Do you think if such a thing happened to you, you would not remember it happening? I would have to say yes you would remember it. But, Knox would always insist it had.

This next interview is available on the Internet; by Ron Patton with Marion Knox. It can be found on www.whale.to/be/knox.html. In this interview Knox responds to Patton's questions as follows-

RP: Can you elaborate further on how the ritual abuse system is formed and how it works?
MK: Well, as I began to work with more survivors, I gathered more details and was able to kind of form a victim's profile. So as I mentioned before, they take a child at approximately three years of age and make the child fast for several days, force the child to witness human sacrifices, and to participate in a cannibalistic communion service. In some instances they physically abuse the child and then place him or her in a cage or coffin to further the trauma. The child is sometimes drowned in a baptismal ceremony and brought

back to life. In the process of all this blasphemy, the child's mind is reversed or shattered into multiplicity. The act of sodomy is also performed to open up the victim's "third eye" which is supposed to enhance psychic ability. During this vial act, a demonic system called, "Legion" is installed. In the King James Bible, Legion is referred to as an, "unclean spirit". This is systematically done to have complete control over the child, like creating a programmed robot.
"A PROGRAMMED ROBOT?" Now come on!

There are survivors still alive from World War II who witnessed things much more horrific and have memories of them still. Some have deep psychological problems, nightmares and such. Most of us have heard of Corrie Ten Boom and the Hiding Place. This was a Traumatic event and they did not forget or "Regress their Memories;" in fact some of them can still remember the faces or their perpetrators 50 years later. Marion claims almost everyone will have no memory of such an event.

Then there is the assertion by Knox you can be programmed at the age of three or four by someone who sodomized you and at a later date can merely say a word and you will just instantly "click" into another personality and commit atrocious acts and then snap back and never remember ever doing it. This they refer to as a triggering mechanism.

Here is another question from the same interview:

RP: How is your therapeutic approach different than others in the area of "deprogramming"?

MK: Well, the key to being healed is the blood atonement of the Lord Jesus Christ. I know a lot of survivors and therapists have a hard time with this because they might have a distorted view of Christianity, but what we are dealing with is in the spiritual realm; it's a spiritual battle between Satan, who wants to steal, kill and destroy as many lives as he possibly can, and, The Lord Jesus Christ, who wants to save and bring healing to the afflicted. I may not have all the details figured out, but I have seen many survivors come to freedom.

You see, the integration route can produce containment, whereas I get to the core of the problem and knock-out the whole MPD system by exposing the lies and secrets with truth and casting the high demons out into the pit. Before I get into the actual deliverance, I listen to their story, take note of their symptoms, and ask a lot of questions. Once it's accurately determined they are ritual abuse victims, I start to investigate deeper by testing the subconscious

199

mind; by the way, and I do it without the use of hypnosis.

Once I locate the highest demon, called the "Strongman", I attempt to cast it out along with Legion. In conjunction with the deliverance, we will sometimes have a Christian communion service but we try not following a ritualistic pattern too much. After the deliverance, there needs to be intensified Christian support should include prayer, friendship, understanding, teaching, counsel, and accountability. The person needs to do whatever it takes to stay away from any relationships and associations, which get in the way of the healing process. I guess it seems too simple for some therapists to understand or comprehend because I have people come to me who have been through conventional psychiatric therapy for years yet I am able to get many of them free, anywhere from a few hours to a couple of days, come back [the MPD]. Eventually, I developed more efficient ways of dealing with this thing Let me give you an example of what occurred with one of the first survivors I was able to help. She was a twin who grew up in Great Falls, Montana and was programmed by Josef Mengele, who she remembered as "Dr. Mingles". Anyway, the unique feature about her, which I never heard about from anyone else

until then, was her mind was programmed
someday her MPD would be reversed so she
could be used as a ruler over many covens within
the Illuminati. So, while working with her I
discovered one of her personalities was
programmed if we would give her a normal
Christian communion service, her MPD would be
reversed. We discussed it some and got approval
from her husband to go along with it. At the end
of the service, she fell over backwards and was
unconscious. About 10 minutes later she woke up
and knew she was no longer multiple. This was
several years ago and it never did and
understanding the larger scope of what all is
involved.

This whole philosophy of Knox and the others is insanity. In this question and answer Knox weaves Christianity into the explanation. This is where he begins to hide behind a cloak of clergy. I regard the Knox's behavior as unintelligent, inconsiderate, and misguided. The answer to this last question is what he told my family happened to them; even though I passed a complete psycho-sexual examination including a thorough polygraph test. He just interjected I would pass such a polygraph test because I was in an altered state of mind when I supposedly committed these acts against my children. Therefore, I could consciously answer the polygraph because I truly did not believe I had done these things and in my mind I did not. One cannot reason with this sort of behavior. They are bent on their teachings, therapy, and counseling without regards to the feelings, emotions, and decency of the individual they claim to be helping.

As I stated earlier in this book; my wife and children are victims in this whole ordeal. I do not want to leave the impression I am tearing them down or downgrading my wife in any way. She was prone; I believe, to accept this counseling due to her mental frame of mind, and her physical ailments left her susceptible to Knox's therapy, counseling and wrong advice. It is difficult to draw a fine line in writing this story. I love my children and in no way or fashion do I want to hurt them further. On the other hand I have to be factual in my approach to writing the story.

Knox usurped his ill gotten false authority and superiority. My wife truly trusted him. Knox gained her trust over time by playing on hurt emotional feelings, which were I believe still present with regards to her father during her childhood and intertwining them with his bogus beliefs.

After gaining her trust, both Knox and Knox's wife were able to lead her down the same path Lacey attempted to lead Diane Lackey down. It is not only Lackey and my wife who had this happen to them, there are dozens of others. There were a handful of times when I would begin to talk and reason with my wife but the Knox's always seemed to be able to commandeer her mind. They never accepted any other explanation for her condition.

The Knox's had her believing I was causing all her ailments and was actually killing her. They were bent on their beliefs and accepted no other. Thankfully Diane Lackey was able to get the needed help via her attorney to clear her head and heart. My attorney did the same along with others, which led me to the proper therapist to determine I did not show the characteristics of a pedophile Knox made me out to be.

The previously mentioned newspaper article from January 2, 2011 has produced a host of responses on the newspapers website.

Here is one from the website www.democratherald.com:

Jodie said on: January 2, 2011, 2:15 pm

We have lived this nightmare for 15 years! In a few short months, our close, loving relationship with our daughter turned into a parent's worst nightmare of hearing accusations of the most horrific kind imaginable! Marion & Doris Knox began counseling our daughter. At first, they talked with her inner, hurt child. They told her as soon as her secrets were out and exposed, there would be a healing service where her inner child would take communion and she would be healed from all the Satanic Ritual Abuse, sexual abuse, Masonic rituals, sodomy and multiple personalities. Marion and Doris did give her inner child communion on several occasions, but the healing never came and the counseling continued. The technique began to change and Marion called up a lot of demons by name and commanded them to tell him ALL kinds of information. These information-gathering sessions sometimes lasted into the early morning hours. Marion & Doris believed they were uncovering Satan's secret strategy as seen in the charts they kept. (Sodomy was the back door to heaven for Satan and evil men, Yahweh Elohim was the master controller in the spirit realm and the Illuminati was very powerful...we, the parents, were accused of being Illuminati members, etc.) (Please Google "Marion Knox

Illuminati" and see all this weird info, which comes up!) In 10 years of observation, we see this as a POWER TRIP. Can you imagine the power in taking a close family by the 'tail' and whirling them around and around at your whim? We were in a Support Group of families devastated by Marion and Doris Knox's counsel for several years in the Portland area. We have met with Knox's former pastors, met with the State of Oregon Investigator for the Psychologists Board, met with Dr. Elizabeth Loftus (known nationwide for her research in false memory syndrome), the False Memory Syndrome Foundation, etc.) We trust all who have their own tragic story will come forward and help put an end to this evil, which has flown under the radar far too long! Someday we want to meet you, Steve Skotko! You are plowing the road for us all! Thank you!

This is what I hope to do, "plow the road" and expose this archaic counseling and therapy for what it really is. It is my desire to see homes healed and relationships reunited. "Evil people prosper, when good people sit back and do nothing;" if you have a story please come forward and be encouraged to heal. This leads us into the next chapter. It is probably the hardest thing I will have to write.

Blurred White by Petra Kratochvil

Chapter Eleven
The Meat of the Allegations

"Confabulation- making up stories to fill in gaps in one's memory" R. Baker

In her book "Confabulations; Creating False Memories – Destroying Families," Eleanor Goldstein talks about inner child therapy and the effects of this type of healing and rehabilitation. She states the following; "So many therapists now practice 'inner child' therapy to the point, they reinforce one another, validating each other's books, and acting as 'expert witnesses' to defend the concept of decades-delayed discoveries from repressed memories of childhood trauma.

Most psychiatrists do not believe in repressed memories. According to David Halperin, psychiatrist at Mount Sinai Hospital in New York, trauma 'is hard to forget.' Sexual abuse is generally an indelible mark on a person. Post Traumatic Stress Disorder (PTSD) creates problems because the memories are impossible to forget. The victims of PTSD do not repress their memories. They cannot get them out of their minds, according to Dr. Halperin.

Therapists who rely so heavily on rediscovered memories do not take into account the traditional scientific knowledge about mind and memory. Memory is made up of fragments, often disjointed and contaminated, some bright and sharp, others murky and vague (refer back to Core Value).

Many memories are additionally contaminated by the images received from television, movies, radio, and books. How can it be determined if a recalled childhood memory is of an event, which actually happened or is a made from TV image? Most rational therapists would treat stories of satanic rituals or crib rape as fantasy. Other therapists believe they must accept any story reported by their clients, however outrageous, as fact and even counsel their clients to take action against their families based on these unsubstantiated stories. To accept a confabulation as accurate revelations is at best non-professional, at worst should be considered criminal malpractice." [1]

Going back to Jodie's post we listed from the newspaper in the previous chapter; I feel your pain and know exactly what you went through.

The beliefs held by Marion Knox and these others, circles around and associates with, inner child therapy, as were described by Jodie. In his interview with Ron Patton, Knox describes the following:

"The perpetrator's goal is to gain power. They believe the devil has the most power, and the most powerful component in the rituals is the blood sacrifices in blasphemy of Christ's atonement. Another very important component is the act of sodomy which is the opposite of the "new birth" we have in Christ.

The ritual abuse system is normally built around a three year old child, because this usually is the optimal time to create dissociation or MPD. This system is actually a mirror image or reflection of what appears to be a shattering of the core personality. They take a child at approximately three years of age and make the child fast for several days, force the child to witness human sacrifices, and to participate in a cannibalistic communion service.

In some instances, they physically abuse the child and then place him or her in a cage or coffin to further the trauma. The child is sometimes drowned in a baptismal ceremony and brought back to life. In the process of all this blasphemy, the child's mind is reversed or shattered into multiplicity.

The act of sodomy is also performed to open up the victim's "third eye" which is supposed to enhance psychic ability. During this vile act, a demonic system called "Legion" is installed. In the King James Bible, Legion is referred to as an, "unclean spirit". This is systematically done to have complete control over the child; in essence creating a programmed robot. The Illuminati belief system says freedom is only obtained through the entrance of true or pure light (sodomy) and life (sacrifice) is only obtained through death.

Now, these survivors have told me the "Key of David" is the Rothschild sodomy. The penetration occurs at an upward angle, so it

209

strikes the nerves at the end of the spine and produces white flashes of light in the brain. They do this on a regular basis; sort of maintenance program to keep everything intact. As a side note, there are Catholic black masses where they sodomize children with a crucifix calling it the "Peace of Mary" because once the dissociation occurs, it almost produces a calming affect; sort of a peaceful feeling." [2]

Personally, I grew up Catholic. I was an altar boy all the way through high school. I never ever was told or heard an inkling of any sort of any type of "black mass" as Knox describes. I have never or was I ever sodomized by a priest and certainly not with a crucifix as he describes. In fact I take offense to such statements. Although, now I am not a practicing catholic, I do have many associates who are and I doubt if I polled them they would ascribe to Knox's accusations.

What is inner child therapy? As the name indicates, this is a method of therapy wherein the Inner Child (We all have one!) can be accessed, and negative conditionings, traumas, etc. can gently and positively be addressed. The Child within all of us is a delightful part of us, a spontaneous, mischievous, sparkling part of our personality. The contra aspect is the child within can throw tantrums, behave unreasonably or inappropriately. Unless there has been childhood trauma and damage, the child within is secondary to the adult personality and controlled by the adult will.

If there has been trauma or damage in childhood, the spontaneous part of us is damaged, and cannot find an outlet. This supposedly deprives us of the enjoyment and fun life should bring. If there has been negative conditioning in childhood and the child was continually told he or she is "Stupid, hopeless, or you will never amount to anything" etc. The adult will always have low self esteem and worth, and never believe they can achieve. If they do achieve, they will class it as an accident, or a lucky mistake, etc. It is important to replace negative childhood conditioning with positive, and to allow the adult personality and will to be in control, not the damaged and defensive child's.[1]

Childhood traumas are often ignored, or "swept under the carpet," by adults around them, more particularly so for adults in mid life stage today. Family bereavements etc were seldom explained to children a few years ago therefore, the child's feelings were never validated, or dealt with. The self worth again is diminished and shadow areas within the psyche established at this stage. Unless these are brought out into the light, looked at, and dealt with, they can be crippling in and the bearer may never achieve their full potential. Childhood abuse of any kind can also be dealt with and much of the fear, low self esteem, inhibition and sadness lifted. Inner child work is a powerful tool indeed and frees and releases hidden agenda areas within, which perpetuate into lifelong unhappiness if not dealt with. [4].

These pseudo-Christian counselors like Knox and those sued by Diane Lackey have ascribed themselves to the theory, which by being sodomized between the ages of two and four years of age you damage "the child" and by the act of sodomy trap the inner child in some sort of stasis within their soul until it can be released at a later date.

The patient (victim) is of course oblivious to this ever happening because they counsel the trauma of such an event as sodomy, when they were small, has been trapped. This is where they teach the victim even though they don't remember, the memory is repressed. Of course only the counselor can help them release the repressed memory. This is what Doris Knox

212

reported in the supplemental police report to the Albany Police.

During the DHS hearing Doris Knox testified she had never said such a thing to the detective. She then was excused and my attorney brought in Dawn Hietala the police detective. When questioned, she was asked to the accuracy of her report; she stated "No I am confident this is what Doris Knox stated to me." The whole interview is on digital recording! Doris Knox perjured herself.

Eleanor Goldstein goes on to say in her book, "Therapists must develop a code of ethics which recognizes accused parents have rights, and repressed memories are not always valid. Books, tapes, and seminars are programmed for specific objectives are improper tools for psychotherapy. Legislators must be aware of the danger of passing laws, which run roughshod over the rights of citizens regarding decades delayed discoveries based on repressed memories. Journalist had better stop, look, and listen before accepting as valid, claims based on repressed memories.

If these agents for justice and opinion-making in our society do not become more responsible, many more abuses will occur, costing our society the very basic ideals it relies on in order to endure, which are fairness and justice. It's time for an appraisal of this dangerous situation by professionals trained in the rational scientific method to look for data and facts about decades delayed discoveries and repressed memories.

It is absolute in this society, where justice is supposed to prevail; parents can be vilified and victimized by their adult children without any recourse. Of course, the adult children are the greatest victims of all. They are sacrificing families, inheritances, and living in fear. New memories have come to dominate their lives." [3]

Prior to ever meeting Marion Knox, my daughter and sons were good loving average children. I have always been proud of them and have always loved them. I could not believe what the "probable cause affidavit," stated as "their words".

After our first encounter with the Knox's as in the way of a bible study in their home, which they still hold on Sunday mornings, my daughter changed dramatically. She did not finish high school but secured her GED. She went on wild binges where we would not hear from her for months at a time, and then finally she is "believed" to have confided in Marion Knox as stated in this same affidavit.

The following is retrieved from the "probable cause affidavit," submitted by Glen Fairall on 09-23-08, Albany Police Case Number 08-20100, starting on Page 8. This document is not available for public reference as all files pertaining to my case were expunged in January 2010. I can only put here what Detective Fairall wrote. I cannot attest to the fact these were the exact words of my daughter or how Fairall expressed them. I am assuming Detective Fairall is stating the truth here, this I take "tongue in cheek."

There are many fabrications in this document as I remember, events and dealings I had with Fairall. He conveniently omitted certain things he told me and stated things in a way "I was to have said." Of course these were incidents when I was not being recorded as in the truck stop parking lot, and the parking lot of the Police Department, how convenient! I cannot be held accountable for his words, only my own. Should these words ever need to be held under public scrutiny I can and will provide a copy of my complete arrest history and my police incarceration.

"Interview with _____ Skotko (daughter), I informed daughter I was recording our conversation in digital audio format (Item

*#6). The following is a condensed summary of
this conversation.*

*"I explained to daughter I had talked with
her mother and brothers and I knew she has
since talked to her mother. Daughter told me her
mother and siblings had been planning to leave
her father for a long time and she had hoped she
would be able to find an apartment, which her
mother and brothers could move into when her
mother finally left her father. She described her
father was a very abusive man and he was
"VERBALLY, EMOTIONALLY, PHYSICALLY,
AND SEXUALLY" abusive. Daughter described
she grew up being yelled at by her father for
everything. She described when she lost her
virginity her father locked her in her bedroom for
a week and would only let her come out to use
the bathroom and only then after she asked
permission. She said her father was always
"VIOLENT AND DRAMATIC"*

*She described from the ages of about six
to sixteen her father made a point of deliberately
watching her whenever she changed her clothing.
Daughter went on to tell me her father has
beaten her and her brother, with sticks or
wooden tools until they broke. Daughter
disclosed there was an incident when she was 14
years old when a boy in the neighborhood whom*

216

she had gotten to know came to her window one night. She said they had gone outside and the boy kissed her. She said the way her father brought her up was such she wasn't allowed to talk to boys and there was to be no physical contact. Daughter said she felt guilty afterwards and told a church counselor about the incident. Daughter described the counselor talked her into telling her parents about the incident with the boy and her father became very angry and contacted the police. She told me nothing really happened between her and the boy and her father became furious. She said her father made it a "HORRIBLE ORDEAL" for her and screamed at her for two days.

Daughter described prior to this incident with the boy her father bought her expensive gifts for no reason and treated her like "HIS LITTLE GIRL." She described a change took place in their relationship. Daughter said it seemed different to her than a normal father and daughter relationship and she was left feeling it was "SICK" and "Twisted."

I asked daughter if she was the victim of sexual abuse. She told me she was a victim of sexual abuse. Although she said she couldn't remember all of the details. Daughter described aside from her father watching her change her

217

*clothes he would also "COP A FEEL
SOMETIMES." Daughter told me it wasn't until
she was older and started going to bars where
men would "COP A FEEL" as her father had
done while she was growing up. She realized
then the touching was wrong. She said, "HE
WAS TOUCHING ME IN AN INAPPROPRIATE
WAY." Daughter would then motion toward her
breasts as she was talking to me about her father
touching her.*

*I asked daughter if there was anything
else, which happened, which went beyond just
touching. She told me "YES". Daughter seemed
to become more upset at this point. She looked as
though she might start to cry. Eventually she
began talking again and told me, "HE'S REALLY
INTO ANAL SEX AND MY MOM WON'T GIVE
HIM THIS...SO I GUESS HE TOOK IT OUT ON
ME." I asked her to explain. Daughter said her
father would come into her bedroom and turn her
onto her side and then he would bend over her
bed and place his penis inside her rectum (anus).*

*Daughter described she was six to eight
years old when her father started anally
sodomizing her. She eventually told me it stopped
when she was about 14 years old. Daughter
described to me she was anally sodomized by her
father on more than ten times in total. She*

*described she could "REMEMBER MORE THAN
TEN TIMES." Daughter went on to tell me about
four or five of incidents occurred in Albany.*

*Daughter described to me these incidents
with her father would happen in the middle of the
night and he would always come into her
bedroom to molest her. She said he never really
spoke to her, other than to tell her to "SHUT
UP." She told me her father would push up her
nightshirt and he would pull down her panties.
She said she had no recollection of the father
using a condom or any type of lubricant.
Daughter told me there were times when she saw
her father's penis during these incidents and
could see his penis was erect. I asked her if her
father's penis is circumcised or uncircumcised.
She told me his penis is circumcised. I asked her
if this was the only time she had ever seen his
penis when she was growing up and she told me
she only saw his penis during the sexual abuse.*

*I then asked daughter if there was
someone else in her family who had been
sexually abusive. She told me she had also been
abused by her grandfather, Charles Owens. This
occurred during visitations to his home in
Indiana. Daughter said she and her brothers
would sleep in the living room of her
grandfather's house, on the couches. Her*

219

grandfather would make an excuse he was checking on them during the night. She said he would "TAKE TURNS'" sexually molesting her and her brother. I asked daughter what her grandfather did to her and she told me it was the same as what her father had done except her grandfather placed her on her stomach. She described her grandfather would also penetrate her vagina and her rectum with his fingers. She said her grandfather never put his penis inside her vagina. I asked her if her grandfather ever talked to her when he was molesting her. She told me her grandfather told her she shouldn't be scared and this would make her a "GOOD GIRL." She said he also told her his penis was his "SNAKE" and this was happening to her was because she was "BAD." Daughter described her grandfather sexually molested her on more than ten times during her childhood and there would be multiple incidents during a single visitation to her grandparents. Daughter estimated she was about four years old the first time and 12 years old the last time her grandfather molested her.

I shut off the recording device and asked daughter if she recalled meeting me in the past. She told me she did remember me and knew I was the police detective she talked to at ABC

220

*HOUSE eight years ago when her father reported the neighborhood boy had come to her window. Daughter told me then she wanted to apologize. I asked her what she wanted to apologize for and she told me, with no prompting from me, she had lied to me at ABC house when she was 14 years old. She said she had lied about the neighborhood boy attempting to rape her because she was so terrified of her father and was so furious when he found out a boy had come to her window at night. She said she thought he would beat her or worse is she told him the truth she had a consensual meeting with a boy during the night. I told daughter I thought I understood her motivation for lying to me when we spoke so many years ago. I told her I would be in touch and she began walking back to her apartment. The case in question was Albany Police Case #01-8177, which occurred in April 2001. **I determined during investigation daughter had not been truthful in her statement about the boy coming to her window during the night attempting to rape her. No arrests were ever made in the case and it was closed.** End of report."*

I love my children so much as I stated earlier in the book, I would give my life for them.

221

On 9-18-08 Doris Knox stated in the supplemental police report my children had no memories of me ever molesting them but they had a "feeling" something happened and it was only during "prayer time" with Marion they supposedly said something to him. On 9-21-08, just three day later, my daughter made all of the above comments to the Police department. It is not so much she made these statements, but they were made with such graphic detail and complexity.

Something here is just not right. Somehow my daughter was brainwashed to all of a sudden say and make all of these accusations, or she was provoked to say these things by my wife or Knox. I have a few comments to make about the statements. I did try whenever possible to give my children nice gifts. As far as I am concerned she is my little girl, my daughter, and always will be no matter what happens. I love her unconditionally. I always tried to protect her. Is this wrong of a father to do? This pains me greatly to have to list all of this information in the detail as was recorded, here in this book.

This report would be to the beholder who reads it to be very disturbing, and it is! However, take into consideration these accusations have followed the same pattern to those of others who have had counseling with Marion Knox and other therapists like them.

During the DHS hearing both my daughter and son were called to testify. Neither of them was able to state anything they reported in the Police Affidavit of arrest. Both showed no emotion. When my daughter was on the stand Susan Juster the DHS investigator sat in her chair and was making the "come on" motions with her hands to encourage my daughter to testify against me. The judge even interjected for her to stop making the motions to encourage a statement. My daughter could not testify to these accusations under oath. Recorded Police interviews however, are not under oath. In court she just sat there and was unable to say anything.

The ABC House is a 501©(3) non-profit organization in Albany, Oregon, which provides a safe, child friendly environment where children who are suspected of having been abused or neglected can come to receive a neutral, objective, comprehensive assessment.

Assessments may include a head to toe medical checkup and/or an interview conducted by specially trained and experienced individuals. Non-offending family members will receive support and information to help their children begin the healing process.

ABC House provides forensic medical exams by a physician who has specific training in child abuse issues and 13 years experience. The program offers a complete assessment of the child's state of health including a complete social and medical history. When necessary children are referred for follow up testing and care with their primary care provider or other specialty providers in the community.

All interviews conducted at the center are digitally recorded for documentation purposes. The ABC House has a forensic interviewer on staff, which has been trained to conduct age appropriate interviews according to best practice. In addition, the forensic interviewer has significant experience and training in child development.

All Law Enforcement and Dept. of Human Service, and Child Protective Workers who conduct interviews at the ABC House receive training in forensic interviewing and meet a standard set according to the local Multi-Disciplinary Team.

The Advocacy program at ABC House provides families with services to help them understand the assessment process children will receive at the center. In addition, the Advocate will work with families to identify any needs they may have to help deal with the current family situation. When appropriate, counseling will be scheduled for children, family members, or if requested, a referral for counseling will be made. Families will also receive information concerning resources available (such as housing, food, shelter from Domestic Violence) when appropriate.

The Advocate assists all eligible families in submitting a Crime Victims Compensation application for help in the following:

COUNSELING: ABC House has a counseling program which focuses on providing healing services not only for children but also family members. The belief of ABC House is children and families need the support and understanding of each other to heal from the abuse a child has suffered. Referrals for outside services are also provided for families when needed or requested. [5]

The staff of the ABC house is professional, thorough, and sensitive to all their patients and the victims of abuse. They pride themselves on "Providing a safe, respectful, and healing environment for children who are victims of abuse."

Dr. Carol Chervenak is Medical Director

and she was called as a witness by me during the DHS hearing in March of 2009. During my daughters previous ordeal as referred to as Albany Police report "Case #01-8177, which occurred in April 2001. *"I (Detective Fairall) determined during the investigation, daughter had not been truthful in her statement about the boy coming to her window during the night attempting to rape her. No arrests were ever made in the case and it was closed. End of report."*

Dr. Carol Chervenak thoroughly examined my daughter in April of 2001 because of the suspicion my daughter had been sexually assaulted at the time, by a boy climbing in her bedroom window at night. Dr. Chervenak also stated at my hearing in March of 2009 my daughter had not been violated in any way. She had not lost her virginity nor were there signs of any physical abuse. In the Affidavit of Arrest Detective Fairall asked my daughter the following; *"I asked daughter if she recalled experiencing any pain? She told me she did recall feeling pain, getting sores around her rectum, and having difficulty having bowel movements."*

This statement points to serious physical signs of abuse! The time frame my daughter was speaking about was between 1998 and 2001. Prior to her examination by the ABC house, which said "there were no signs of abuse." I now ask you the reader to put it together. Who is telling the truth? Also as a result of this questioning of my daughter the arrest record was as such:

The District Attorney of Linn County, State of Oregon, accuses the above named defendant Stephan John Skotko of the offenses, Case #08091915

Count 1, Sodomy in the first degree. (FSG-9; A Felony; ORS 163.405) FPC#: 45173356 "The defendant, on or before January 1, 1998 to September 21, 2001, in Linn County, Oregon, did unlawfully and knowingly engage in deviate sexual intercourse with Daughter Skotko, a person under 16 years of age and the child of the said defendant.

Count 2, Sodomy in the first degree. (FSG-9; A Felony; ORS 163.405) FPC#: 45173356 "The defendant, on or before January 1, 1998 to September 21, 2001, in Linn County, Oregon, did unlawfully and knowingly engage in deviate sexual intercourse with Daughter Skotko, a person under 16 years of age and the child of the said defendant.

Count 3, Sodomy in the first degree. (FSG-9; A Felony; ORS 163.405) FPC#: 45173356 "The defendant, on or before January 1, 1998 to September 21, 2001, in Linn County, Oregon, did unlawfully and knowingly engage in deviate sexual intercourse with Daughter Skotko, a person under 16 years of age and the child of the said defendant.

Count 4, Sodomy in the first degree. (FSG-9; A Felony; ORS 163.405) FPC#: 45173356. The defendant, on or before January 1, 1998 to September 21, 2001, in Linn County, Oregon, did unlawfully and knowingly engage in deviate sexual intercourse with Daughter Skotko, a person under 16 years of age and the child of the said defendant.

Count 5, Sexual Abuse in the first Degree. (FGS-8, B felony; ORS 163.427(1A)) FPC#: 45173356. The defendant, on or before January 1, 1998 to September 21, 2001, in Linn County, Oregon, did unlawfully and knowingly subject Daughter Skotko to sexual contact.

Count 6, INCEST (FGS-1; C Felony; ORS 163.525) FPC#:45173356. The defendant, on or

before January 1, 1998 to September 21, 2001, in Linn County, Oregon, did unlawfully and knowingly engage in deviate sexual intercourse with Daughter Skotko, a person under 16 years of age and the child of the said defendant, either legitimately or illegitimately, as a descendant of either the whole or half blood; contrary to the statutes and against the peace and dignity of the State of Oregon.
Dated this day: September 24, 2008
By: Ani Yardumian, OSB # 94470; Deputy District Attorney.
Trial attorney for the State: Ani Yardumian, OSB # 94470

Now had I perpetrated all these crimes in 2001, which I did not, I am sure the ABC house would have found evidence of these crimes in their examination of 2001, which was near the end of the time listed in my arrest; at which time someone would have been arrested in April of 2001.

At my DHS hearing in 2009, Dr. Cherveniak further stated "no abuse had occurred against my daughter at the time of the examination in 2001."

Second, The Albany Police Department had in their possession at the time of my arrest in

2008, a complete medical record from the ABC house, a DVD video of Detective Fairall's interview with my daughter, and statements from everyone concerned, along with a statement of Detective Fairall in My Arrest Affidavit, which he believed my daughter of not speaking the truth. Yet Detective Fairall still arrested me and charged me with these crimes, which were proven medically as to not of happening from the periods of 1998- 2001.

I hope this sheds some light onto the insanity of all these allegations. Not only did they not happen and the accusations were a result of brain washing, but there is solid, hard-core, medical evidence and testimony under oath it could not have happened and again, it did not happen!

Notes Chapter 11

[1] Eleanor Goldstein (1992), Confabulations-
Creating False Memories, SRS Books,
      Boca Raton, Florida. P 329-330, pp 3.
[2] http://www.whale.to/b/knox_h.html pp 14.
Retrieved August 1, 2009
[3] Eleanor Goldstein (1992), Confabulations-
Creating False Memories, SRS Books,
      Boca Raton, Florida. P 330-331, pp 2-7.
[4] http://www.aest.org.uk/innerchild/what-is-
innerchild-therapy.php. Retrieved   January 7,
2011
[5] http://abchouse.org Retrieved January 7, 2011

Blurred lights by Petra Kratochvil

Chapter Twelve
The Fight Continues
By Stephan Skotko and Teila Tankersley

"If you are going through hell, keep going."
Winston Churchill

With the letter I received from the DHS regarding "their concerns" of a threat to my youngest son; I plowed ahead with my life. I received the letter in January 2009 while still reuniting with my family in Ohio, where I now reside.

The fight continued as 2009 became a

232

reality. My family opened their arms and received me back. Reflecting back on this time now; I had to have been in shock with what had happened. Daily life was so taxing and exhausting. It seemed as if living took all the strength from my mind, body, and soul. It is so hard to try and put into words exactly how you feel when enduring this type of ordeal.

Over the previous twenty-five years of marriage there was never one incident of abuse in any way shape or form. The police were never contacted to any sort of domestic violence in our home and lives.

My three children were born in Colorado Springs where my wife and I met, dated, were married and raised our two oldest children for the first part of their lives. We had love in our home. We were happy there. We moved to Oregon in January of 1998 and the whole time in Oregon there was no trouble, abuse, or domestic violence of any sort. We left Colorado Springs because my wife had wanted to distance ourselves from my stepson; my wife's son from her previous marriage.

I had noticed changes in her after my youngest son was born in 1996. She felt as if my stepson would badly influence my younger children. I did not share her sentiment. My stepson had worked for me for a number of years and was an excellent employee. I was opposed to forcing him out and on his own. We had a large house with a basement, which had two bedrooms and a full bathroom, separate from the rest of the home. I used one of the bedrooms in the basement as my business office and the other was his bedroom.

He was a good kid and I enjoyed raising him after my marriage to his mother. He had a good heart, he was considerate, and all around he was a good person. The thing I admired about him was he was considerate of other people and had respect for them. When the police interviewed my wife prior to my arrest she had made some comments about my stepson, which did not make sense to me.

Then again, the whole ordeal did not make sense. The whole police report was riddled with inaccuracy. A definite sign of the brainwashing she endured. I was opposed to having my stepson leave us, just at a time when he was getting ready to really excel in life. But, my wife insisted he leave and move out.

In fact one night in Colorado Springs prior to us leaving for Oregon, the two of them had a very heated and loud discussion. When I came home my little kids were crying in their bedrooms and scared. As I came home my stepson was leaving. I believe now she confronted him about him moving out of the house.

In the Police Affidavit of my arrest it states the following, (Detective Fairall speaking): "Wife told me her son (my stepson) who is 33years old has never told her he was abused by Stephan Skotko. However, Wife said stepson hates Stephan Skotko deeply and she does not know why. She described Stephan Skotko had adopted stepson but stepson changed his name back to his biological father's name even though his biological father has never had any contact with him.

She said she doesn't currently know how to get in contact with her son and she last knew he and his wife were living somewhere in Colorado Springs. She said her family; including stepson had been involved in a cult like church called 'Victory Chapel' now known as 'Victory World Outreach' in Colorado Springs.

She said when she and Stephan Skotko left the church her son and his wife chose to stay and this was why they have not had much contact. She said in past months, she has been contacted by "Bill Collectors" who were looking for stepson."

My wife's sentiments about the church in Colorado Springs are not those of mine. We moved away from Colorado Springs because of her feelings about my stepson and those of the church. I was attempting to keep peace in my home and reflecting back now can see my wife was already not able to deal with the daily pressures of life.

When the doctor at OHSU told us her tumor was eleven years old I did not realize the significance of His statement. Now, I go back eleven years in my mind from the date of her surgery; eleven years takes me right to this time frame when we were leaving Colorado Springs and her feelings about my stepson. I can see clearly now the age of her tumor coincides with when she began to show signs of making irrational decisions.

I remained in Ohio until January 25th, 2009 and then went back to Oregon to prepare for the impending DHS hearing. The State of Oregon wanted to terminate my parental rights forever. The District attorney did not have enough solid evidence to even invoke a grand jury indictment when criminal charges were pending against me back in November of 2008. I believe now it all fell through the cracks because of the similarities in regards to the incident with

Mr. McCracken in 2002 and the involvement of Knox.

I also believe they knew it would never go to court, if it did, it would never make it past a jury, so I believe they figured a DHS hearing, which had only a judge had a better chance of success. In this way they would only need to convince one person of my guilt instead of a jury of 12. They would come to find out later this was also a terrible mistake.

During the period between January and April of 2009, I was able to make contact with a support group in Portland, Oregon. As it played out these people were not able to really help me. The one thing, which came out of this meeting, was they would inform me, and I would be introduced to Dr. Kirk Johnson in Vancouver Washington. Dr. Johnson is a psychologist. He works with these types of cases and is well respected in the Pacific Northwest. He was the doctor who performed a complete psycho-sexual examination on me.

This examination was my idea through my attorney. I voluntarily took it. As Dan my attorney put it, "Steve if you did not do anything, you have nothing to fear." How true this statement is. However, still lingering in the back of my mind was all the things said about me, and the accusations. In my mind the thoughts went back and forth, "what if I did have MPD or DID as they claimed." I decided to subject myself to a whole day of tests.

Before Dr. Johnson even did the examination he did a thorough interview of me and all the things I ever did and could remember since I was a child. This was difficult. There are things from my childhood, which I am ashamed of. I think we all have things we did or said which we are all ashamed of. After interviewing me for about an hour and a half, he then sent me to see Steven Norton.

Steven Norton is a certified polygraph examiner and retired from the police department. The polygraph examination lasted around an hour. During the time previous to the polygraph examination Steven Norton thoroughly interviewed me as did Dr. Johnson. The results of the examination are as follows:

EXAMINATION:

Based upon the information obtained a Zone Comparison Test was developed. The examination was conducted on a Lafayette LX4000 Computerized Polygraph Instrument with PolyScore. The questions were mixed to provide for a clear evaluation. Relevant questions were as follows:

1. Did you even once put your penis in Daughter's anus?

Answer. No.

2. Have you even one time touched your daughter in a sexual way?

Answer: No.

3. Do you ever require your daughter to change her clothes in front of you?

Answer: No.

Based upon the subject's lack of physiological response to the relevant questions, it is this examiner's opinion Stephen was not attempting deception when he answered no to the relevant questions. It should be noted Steve volunteered there was an incident where Caroline had called to him and he had gone into her room and she was only wearing her bra, but he's never required her to change her clothes in front of him. He insists he's never touched her sexually. At the conclusion of the first exam a second exam was conducted regarding ever having anal contact with his oldest son or had sexual contact with him. Relevant questions were as follows:

1. Did you ever anally penetrate his Anus?

Answer: No.

2. Did you ever touch your son in a sexual way?

Answer: No.

*Based on two charts, it is this examiner's opinion
Mr. Skotko was not attempting deception when he
answered no to these relevant questions.
During post-test interview, Stephen made no
additional admissions.
I found nothing, which would preclude a valid
examination.*

*Respectfully Submitted,
Steven A. Norton
Certified Polygraph Examiner
SAN/jkn*

I cannot put into words how humiliating
this experience was. I cannot put into words how
I felt as this man asked me these types of
questions concerning my children. I felt like a
total failure. I felt as if someone or something
came into my heart and just ripped "fatherhood"
from my life. It was evil and ugly. It was like a
huge creature entered my life and was just
swallowing up my manhood. I felt totally
defeated.

After the interview I asked Steven Norton
if I could see the chart, which was on a computer
screen and he eagerly showed me everything. He
also stated, "it is not on the report but the
computer diagnostics for the test stated there was

less than 1/10 of 100th chance at deception."
This says it is certain 99.99% I was not trying
deception.

When I left Steven Norton's office he
shook my hand and stated. "It's good to shake an
honest man's hand." He also told me, "If anyone
is guilty of the things you have been accused of
they would want to be nowhere close to this
machine." I then left to return to Dr. Johnson's
office. Before I did I sat there in my vehicle and
just cried and cried.

I prayed and poured out my heart to God
for forgiveness from having not protected my
family from the "devil" I felt was just ripping my
life to shreds. It was ripping my children from
my life. I love my children so much. I never did
anything to hurt them and I was being led down
this path of life, which I did not want to go.
Anything, which could be burned up in my life
was up till then.

Right then and there is where I started to
come out of "The Fog." I believe this is where I
began my life again. Again, this is where I could
look back and only see one set of footprints in the
sand, and they were not mine. I know beyond a
shadow of a doubt God himself was carrying me
through all of this. Whenever I needed a miracle I
received one. It was during this time I felt so

alone, so worthless, as if no one in this world cared for me.

While I was sitting under the canopy of Mark Christman's home in Stayton, Oregon, I got one of those miracles. Mark was kind to rent me a room from January 2009 until September 2009. While there I was sitting under the canopy and I just prayed, "God I am so lonely I need someone to talk to." A few minutes later I received a phone call from my friend John Seifker in Albany.

John is a missionary evangelist who travels a lot to South America. He said to me "Steve this is John, Its going to be alright. You are going to make it." So you ask me, how is this a miracle? Well at the time John was in Peru, trekking through the jungle. He has an international phone, which he uses for emergencies.

He went on to say. "Normally I don't get a single solitary signal in this part of the country and this far into the jungle, but my interpreter who was looking at the phone said to me, 'Juan you have a signal a strong one, you should call your friend Steve, I have been thinking of him and praying as we have been walking!'" My friend this is a miracle and a way, in which God showed me He was with me and heard my prayer!

The whole process of the psychosexual examination cost me in the neighborhood of $5,000.00, this included Dr. Johnson testifying in person at the DHS hearing. An interesting thing Dr. Johnson told me was in all his work and research conducted in the area of pedophilia the perpetrator never changed sexes. This means they either molest girls or they molest boys, never ever both. Also with a certainty, a perpetrator of pedophilia never engages in sexual activity with adults while engaging in pedophilia. So in a weak sort of way, this was good news. He also testified to this at the hearing.

This was it, all the finances were gone or in trust with my attorney. From this moment forward, I literally lived day to day and by faith. It was pretty amazing at how I made it. I enrolled in every government program I thought would help me. I had claimed some equipment from my business and sold most of it to pay my way. My income tax refund came in and my family in Ohio helped out when they could, they were great. Every little thing like this happened at the right time. Those were more of the daily miracles I experienced along the way and still do. I remained in Oregon until September of 2009, when I drove back to Ohio permanently..

Preparing for the DHS hearing in March of 2009 was difficult. There were so many things I was struggling with and now my own wife and children were going to take me to trial. The hearing lasted for a day and a half. During, which time my two older children would testify, my wife, myself, Doris Knox, Marion Knox, Dr. Johnson, Dr. Chervenak from the ABC house in Albany, Oregon, and both police detectives. This was all explained in the previous chapter. During these months prior to the hearing I was required to attend mandatory pre-divorce counseling for the welfare of my youngest child.

In October of 2008, my wife had filed divorce papers. Those divorce papers had 4 different forms of handwriting meaning four different people had at some point spent time filling out the paperwork. She did not show for this meeting. We also had a mandatory meeting with a marriage mediator; she did not show for this appointment either.

The month and a half prior to my hearing were filled with back and forth telephone calls from my attorney and I was jumping through hoops. I was also going through a variety of physical, emotional and psychological examinations, which were required by the courts. My attorney depositioned my wife at this time. It was during this same time, I was forced to begin filing for bankruptcy.

So much was happening and the stress I experienced was overwhelming. I remember waking up one Sunday morning with horrible chest pains. I drove all the way to Portland Oregon to the VA Hospital's emergency room.

They ran all kinds of tests. A Psychologist finally came in and talked to me before I left to return home. I told her everything, which I had been experiencing. They all determined I was under a huge amount of stress and was on the verge of a panic attack.

When I was getting ready to leave I overheard one nurse tell another; "Poor guy, he just has a broken heart." She hugged me before I left. I really feel this did more for me at the time than any medicine or test ever could. I never got her name, and for the life of me would not remember her today if I saw her. But, if she ever reads this book; I want to say thank you to her. She will never know how much the hug helped me. You go right on hugging people and showing love, it makes a huge difference in ways you will never know!

Reflecting back, I am amazed and I have learned a tremendous amount about repressed memories. All the research for this book has shed a tremendous amount of light on this subject. It is alarming how easily counselors and therapists can manipulate a person to "remember things, which never happened." It is so easy to implant false memories into someone battling through abuse and hurt. So many things have transpired over the first decade of the new millennium regarding repressed memories and (RMT). So what is repressed memories all about. How can it change the course of good people's lives? My co-author has the following to add

Here is some basic history on what repressed memory therapy is. "While all this is taught in introductory psychology courses and has been taken by novelists and screenwriters to be a truism; Freud's repression theory has never been verified by rigorous scientific proof." –John Hockmann (Schacter).

What is "Repressed Memory Therapy" exactly? It is based on a theory, in which a patient presenting problems, such as depression, marital problems and or even an eating disorder had more than likely at one time in their life been a victim of sexual abuse and the event or events were so traumatic, the patient represses the memory.

In reality, the truth is many choose not to dwell on unpleasant experiences and make an effort to erase negative memories from their minds. A human being actually has the ability to forget things because they were never encoded properly or because neural connections have been destroyed and/or because they've chosen to forget them. But, there is little scientific evidence to support the notion traumatic experiences are typically unconsciously repressed or unconscious memories of traumatic events are significant casual factors in physical or mental illness (Schacter).

Dr. McHugh wrote in 1992, "These practices will eventually be discredited, and this epidemic will end in the same way, which the witch trials ended in Salem. But time is passing, many families are being hurt, and confidence in the competence and impartiality of psychiatry is eroding." Dr. McHugh concludes. "psychiatric thought gone awry, fueled by social factors, is a recurring event in the history of psychiatry." He cautions history should teach psychiatry is capable of "glorious medical triumphs and hideous medical mistakes." However, the practice continued.....

The fact of the matter is many psychologists have indeed concluded their colleagues, which are practicing this repressed memory therapy (RMT) are actually encouraging, prodding, and suggesting false memories of abuse to their patients. To top it all off, many of these recovered memories are of being sexually abused by parents, grandparents, and ministers and believe it or not sometimes-even aliens. Many of those accused claim the memories are false and have sued therapists for their alleged role in creating false memories, rightfully so, because this unscientific theory is destroying families and creating falsehoods.

In 1994, Dr. Elizabeth Loftus showed not only is it possible to implant false memories, but it is relatively easy to do so. It is as unlikely all recovered memories of childhood sexual abuse are false as they are all true. What is known about memory makes it especially difficult to sort out truth from distorted or false recollections.

However, some consideration should be given to the fact certain brain processes are necessary for any memories to occur. Memories of infant abuse or of abuse, which took place while the child was unconscious, are unlikely to be accurate. Memories, which have been directed by dreams or hypnosis, are also unreliable. Dreams as we all know might very well feel real however, they are not always accurate. Furthermore, the data of dreams is generally ambiguous.

Obviously it would be unconscionable to ignore accusations of sexual abuse. But it is also inhumane to encourage patients to recall memories of sexual abuse if they did not occur. Assuming all or most emotional problems are due to repressed memories of childhood sexual abuse, it still would not be considered ethical to encourage delusional beliefs. Assuming if you can't disprove a patient was sexually abused shouldn't be the proof they were. A responsible therapist has a duty to help a patient sort out delusion from reality, dreams and confabulations from truth, and real abuse from imagined abuse.

Hundreds and hundreds of credible psychologists have presented reasons as to why "repressed memory therapy" should not be used, yet, the fact remains it is still being practiced; in the hands of a mad man, this therapy is dangerous! "Professor Richard McNally from Harvard University was quoted as saying the theory of repressed memories was "the most pernicious bit of folklore ever to infect psychology and psychiatry."

An organization called, "Stop bad therapy" has concluded, repressed memory therapy is dangerous, and it has been shown memory recovery therapy increases the rate of suicidal ideation, hospitalization, self-mutilation, and divorce. So, why is this type of therapy allowed to exist? (End of Teila's information).

If formally educated counselors and therapists have come to these conclusions what damage could be done to an individual whose counselor or therapist is a lay pseudo-Christian counselor who is not formally educated and not government controlled or submitted to any sort of authority? I have done my own research on Satanic Ritual Abuse and the Hysteria behind it. You mix (RMT) with the Satanic Ritual Abuse (SRA) hysteria, which struck the nation in the 1980's and 1990's and you have a witch's brew laced with poison. I discovered the following about (SRA).

Satanic ritual abuse (SRA, sometimes known as ritual abuse, ritualistic abuse, organized abuse, sadistic ritual abuse and other variants) refers to a moral panic, which originated in the United States in the 1980s, spreading throughout the country and eventually too many parts of the world, before subsiding in the late 1990s. Allegations of (SRA) involved reports of physical and sexual abuse of individual in the context of occult or satanic rituals. At its most extreme definition, SRA involved a worldwide conspiracy involving the wealthy and powerful of the world elite in which children were abducted or bred for sacrifices, pornography, and prostitution, (Rothchilds).

Nearly every aspect of SRA was controversial, including its definition, the source of the allegations and proof thereof; including testimonials of alleged victims, and court cases involving the allegations and criminal investigations.

The panic affected lawyers, therapists', and social workers' handling of allegations of child sexual abuse. Allegations initially brought together widely dissimilar groups, including religious fundamentalists, police investigators, child advocates, therapists, and clients in psychotherapy. The movement gradually secularized, dropping or deprecating the "satanic" aspects of the allegations in favor of names, which were less overtly religious such as "sadistic" or simply "ritual abuse," thus, becoming more associated with dissociative identity disorder (DID) and government conspiracy theories.

The panic was influenced to a large extent by testimony of children and adults, which was obtained using therapeutic and interrogation techniques now considered discredited. Initial publicity generated was by the now-discredited autobiography Michelle Remembers (1980), and sustained and popularized throughout the decade by the McMartin preschool trial.

Testimonials, symptom lists, rumors, and techniques to investigate or uncover memories of SRA were disseminated through professional, popular, and religious conferences, as well as through the attention of talk shows, which sustained and spread the moral panic further throughout the United States and beyond.

In some cases allegations resulted in criminal trials with varying results; after seven years in court, the McMartin trial resulted in no convictions for any of the accused, while other cases resulted in lengthy sentences. Scholarly interest in the topic slowly built, eventually resulting in the conclusion the phenomenon was a moral panic.

Official investigations produced no evidence of widespread conspiracies or of the slaughter of thousands sacrificed in satanic rituals held in the backwoods of remote country sides. Only a small number of verified crimes have even remote similarities to tales of SRA. In the latter half of the 1990s interest in SRA declined and skepticism became the default position, with only a minority of believers giving any credence to the existence of SRA. [1]

It is this precise mix of Repressed Memories, Satanic Ritual Abuse, and their own unproved theories of Joseph Mengele and Aleister Crowley, which DePaoli, Knox, Lacey and the others base their therapy on. Dyan Lackey won a lawsuit against all except Knox. Spice it up and hide it under the guise of religion and they can virtually go undetected and not be accountable to any government or federal agency. These listed reside in Oregon. One wonders what can and does transpire across the rest of the country.

Initial accusations were made in the context of the rising political power of conservative Christianity within the United States, [2] and religious fundamentalists were enthusiastic in promoting rumors of SRA. [3] Psychotherapists who were actively Christian began advocating for the diagnosis of dissociative identity disorder (DID) and soon after accounts similar to Michelle Remembers began to appear, with some therapists believing the alters of some patients were the result of demonic possession.[4]

Protestantism was instrumental in starting, spreading and maintaining rumors through sermons about the dangers of SRA, lectures by purported experts and prayer sessions, including showings of the 1987 Geraldo Rivera television special. [5] Secular proponents began to appear, and child protection workers became significantly involved. Law enforcement trainers, many themselves strongly religious, became strong promoters of the reality of the claims and became self-described "experts" on the topic.

Their involvement in child sexual abuse cases produced more allegations of SRA, adding credibility to the phenomenon. [2] As the explanations for SRA were distanced from evangelical Christianity and into the realm of "survivor" groups, the motivations ascribed to purported Satanists shifted from combating a religious nemesis to mind control and abuse as an end to itself.[6]

Clinicians, psychotherapists and social workers documented clients alleging histories of SRA [6] though the claims of therapists were unsubstantiated beyond the testimonies of their clients. [6] One explanation for the SRA allegations is they were based upon false memories caused by the over-use of hypnosis and other suggestive techniques by therapists underestimating the suggestibility of their clients.[7]

The altered state of consciousness induced by hypnosis rendered patients unusually able to produce confabulations, often with the assistance of their therapists.[8] Advocates of false memory syndrome (FMS), a controversial term promoted by the False Memory Syndrome Foundation, claim the purported "memories" of ritual abuse are actually false memories, created iatrogenically through suggestion or coercion.[9]

The FMSF has used the idea of ritual abuse as a strategy to illustrate their position, in which most allegations of sexual abuse uncovered by the suggestive techniques used during recovered memory therapy are false "memories" of events, which never happened. According to Kathleen Faller this has contributed to the sensationalization of the ritual abuse cases in the media.[10]

Paul R. McHugh, professor of psychiatry at Johns Hopkins University discusses in his book Try to Remember, the developments, which led to the creation of false memories in the SRA moral panic and the formation of the FMSF as an effort to bring contemporary scientific research and political action to the polarizing struggle about false memories within the mental health disciplines.

According to McHugh, there is no coherent scientific basis for the core belief of one side of the struggle. Sexual abuse can cause massive systemic repression of memories, which can only be accessed through hypnosis, coercive interviews, and other dubious techniques. The group of psychiatrists who promoted these ideas, whom McHugh terms "Mannerist Freudians", consistently followed a deductive approach to diagnosis in which the theory and causal explanation of symptoms was assumed to be childhood sexual abuse leading to dissociation, followed by a set of unproven and unreliable treatments with a strong confirming inevitably produced the allegations and causes, which were assumed to be there.[1]

The treatment approach involved isolation of the patient from friends and family within psychiatric wards dedicated to the treatment of dissociation, filled with other patients who were treated by the same doctors with the same flawed methods and staff members who also coherently and universally ascribed to the same set of beliefs. These methods began in the 1980s and continued for several decades until a series of court cases and medical malpractice lawsuits resulted in hospitals failing to support the approach. In cases where the dissociative symptoms were ignored, the coercive treatment approached ceased and the patients were removed from dedicated wards. Allegations of satanic rape and abuse normally ceased. "Recovered" memories were identified as fabrications and conventional treatments for presenting symptoms were generally successful.[1]

All the hysteria, all the media coverage, all the sermons preached in churches, and all of it came down to being identified as "fabrications." I believe numbers of individuals "power tripped" to gain notoriety for themselves and took advantage of the situation and hysteria. It became a "feeding frenzy," in both the religious and secular worlds. Christian's went on a power trip, all wanting to be like Jesus to have the power to cast out demons. I believe this is the same type of "power trip and quest for control," in which Knox and these others function under.

Politicians went on a power trip to get elected and build political empires. We witnessed news reporters conducting shows for ratings; all this at the hands of innocent people suffering with some sort of ailment or mental handicap. In most cases innocent people suffered and their lives forever changed because of somebody's quest for power and attainment of ill gotten superiority and control.

How many families such as my own have been ripped to shreds because somebody falsely attained their superiority; exercised their will, and preyed on those who appeared to be weaker?

In most cases the only flaw of those who appeared to be weaker was they had good and trusting hearts. More than ever we need all counselors, religious or secular, to be required to adhere to a code of ethics and to be properly educated. If they violate these ethics, we need to hold them to the fire and being accountable.

I draw huge similarities to the research I did on Tuskegee. They knew they were causing pain and suffering, yet they continued. They pursued the treatment with reckless abandon. There is testimony after testimony coming in as to the therapy and counseling performed by Knox and these others, which is so similar. Case after case presents the same therapy, with the same outcome.

As we write the words for this book we are receiving emails from families and individuals devastated by this therapy. This not only happened amongst those in Oregon but further investigation reveals it is happening all over the country; the same therapy and counsel, with the same outcome. In my opinion, repressed memory treatment is no different than the barbaric experiments our government undertook at Tuskegee. It is the same devil, the same spirit; it's just the devil is wearing a different mask. How long will our society and the government let these get away with what they do, with no consequences for their actions?

Notes Chapter 12:

[1] McHugh, PR (2008). Try to Remember: Psychiatry's Clash over Meaning,   Memory and Mind. Dana Press. ISBN 978-1932594393

[2] Donner GJ; Bottoms BL; Najdowski CN (2009). Children as Victims, Witnesses, and Offenders: Psychological   Science and the Law. New York: Guilford Press. pp. 81–101. ISBN 1-60623-332-7.

[3] Jenkins P (1992). Intimate enemies: moral panics in contemporary Great Britain. New York: Aldine de Gruyter.   pp. 151–76. ISBN 0-202-30435-3

[4] Spanos NP (1996). Multiple Identities & False Memories: A Sociocognitive   Perspective American   Psychological Association. pp. 269–285. ISBN 1-55798-340-2.

[5] Victor, 1993, p. 46-7 & 68-70

[6] Frakfurter, D (2003). "The satanic ritual abuse panic as religious-studies data".

[7] Loftus & Ketcham, 1996, p. 85

[8] Ellis, Bill (2000). Raising the devil: Satanism, new religions, and the media.   Lexington, KY: University Press of   Kentucky. pp. 87–97. ISBN 0-81312170-1.

[9] Fraser, GA (1997). The Dilemma of Ritual Abuse: Cautions and Guides *for Therapists*. American Psychiatric Publishing, Inc. pp. 105–117. ISBN 0880484780.

[10] Faller, 2003, p. 51

Snowy Road by Petr Kratochvil

Chapter Thirteen
Steve Begins Sharing his story
By Teila Tankersley

"Trust in the LORD with all your heart and lean not on your own understanding; In all your ways submit to him, and he will make your paths straight." Proverbs 3:5-6

What do you do, when a friend you haven't seen for two decades tells you and your husband his wife and children had taken him to court accusing him of sodomy? Well, for one thing, you ask him what happened. You pre-

261

determine in your mind if the accusations are true you want nothing to do with him. Although Steve was ready to share his story, he was still apprehensive. He had no idea as to where or how to begin. The accusations alone had scarred him for so long: yet with an honest and open heart he began sharing his story with me. He spoke about the accusations, Marion Knox, and the court case. He also began showing me court documentations and paperwork he had accumulated throughout this time.

In a quiet voice he began describing what it was like as he heard for the first time the accusations against him. Steve was devastated and all he could think was what on earth are they talking about? Steve was even more stunned when officers handcuffed and locked him up. As he was relaying all those past events to me, I couldn't help but notice even in hindsight he was finding it still hard to believe this really happened. It was a nightmare he never wants any one to have to go through.

He remembered thinking at any moment his wife would come to her senses, call him, and this would all be behind them. But, this never happened. During this entire ordeal, Steve was unable to see or to speak to his wife and children except on a few occasions. He was able to see her in the courtroom, even then they were separated by their lawyers. It was a long drawn out process, which extended out over the course of several months.

Steve knew the accusations were not true, he felt helpless and alone. Few people knew what this family was going through. The ordeal was clearly a traumatizing event for all parties. Steve's wife and his children were listening to the guidance of their counselor, Marion Knox to get them through this. Steve was clinging to his lawyer's advice and telling as few souls as possible. The court process dragged on and in the meantime because of the pending charges Steve was unable to continue working at his present job. He found it nearly impossible to find work.

Considering his sanity, Steve said he finally confided in a few close friends and family. He used this time to begin educating himself on the theory of repressed memories. He was attempting to make sense of everything happening. In the meantime, Knox was busy trying to convince the courts these charges were factual. Knox tried to explain although Steve, his wife, and the children did not have any memory of the events. All this was due to repressed memories.

Thankfully, Steve's lawyer helped to connect him with a few families who had gone through similar experiences with Knox. This brought him strength, but the court process was taking its toll on him. He lost his own business, his family, his confidence, and his desire to go on living. However, he knew he had to continue to fight, so the truth would be made known. Trying to keep his mind busy and to plan for the future, Steve enrolled in College. The structure and the assignments took his mind off some of the stress and madness. He discovered himself regaining some of his confidence.

In November of 2008, criminal charges were dismissed. In March of 2009, he was successfully defended in his DHS hearing. But sadly Steve's dream of being reunited with his wife and family did not happen. Steve's wife, still under Marion Knox's influences, filed for divorce. The restraining orders granted to his wife remained in effect and stayed in place until September of 2010.

This was a whole year after he left Oregon and moved to Ohio. The Oregon DHS still obstinate after failing to find cause against Steve blocked any effort by Steve to even have supervised telephone visitation with his youngest son. I questioned Steve about this and he told me,

"All I wanted to do was tell my son, I love him. They would not even permit me to do this." His son's court appointed attorney told Steve's attorney Steve would need to file a formal complaint and go back to court and get the judge's approval and court order for this since the divorce was still pending. A process, which would have cost in the neighborhood of $10,000.00

The entire time Steve shared his story with me, he was extremely protective over his wife. He explained Marion Knox took advantage of her. She was vulnerable and had been ill for a while. Steve continually referred to her and the children as victims as well. Gale Millard has been a dear friend throughout this entire nightmare and was quite a comfort to Steve. Gale himself was familiar with Knox and at one point Knox had even tried to convince Gale he also had been a victim of a repressed memory. Gale wasn't falling for it. Instead, Gale dismissed Knox as simply a mad man and never had anything to do with him from this moment forward. He soon after was filed with a restraining by his wife. His marriage also ended in divorce.

Seeing the turmoil this all had taken on Steve and knowing all the hours Steve had spent investigating this "RMT" theory, Gale began encouraging Steve to write a book about his experiences and to blow the lid off this unorthodox therapy.

This gave Steve the confidence to slowly begin opening up to his friends and to begin sharing his story and his experience. It was shortly after this my husband and I had learned Steve and his wife were going through a divorce. It would be another two or three months before Steve would confide in us his story. Upon hearing it we also agreed his story needed to be told. I volunteered to help Steve write this book.

Repressed Memory therapy is nothing new, in fact I had heard about "RMT" a few years back. A dear friend of mine, Susan, had confided in me she had gone to a counselor in her teen years. Susan confided in me she had started in therapy because she'd been depressed. Her parents took her to see a couple of different therapists, but it wasn't until she began seeing a therapist, which specialized in repressed memories her nightmare truly began.

She knew her brother had molested her. But, her therapist didn't think it was important or unusual. It was rarely even mentioned, except to point out her brother must have learned the sexual abuse from her father. Under probing, suggestions, and hypnosis, she was "asked" if something else had happened. She was told if her brother molested her, her brother must have learned it from someone in the house—her father. She was told over and over she was avoiding the truth, and by avoiding the truth she'd never get better.

She was told the whole reason she was sick and depressed was because she wasn't processing things correctly. If she wanted to get better, then she needed to trust the therapist and "the process" (whatever this meant). She was told it was "normal" not to have any memories of the abuse. Now, this of course was not the counselor Steve, his wife, and the children were seeing. However, I noted there were similarities, and it wasn't right.

My friend Susan eventually confronted her father accusing him of abuse because the therapist over time had convinced Susan her father had to of abused her. The actual perpetrator went un-confronted. The more I read on repressed memories and the more individuals I spoke to on this topic, it became apparent it didn't matter what the individuals thought prior to counseling. By the time they were done they had believed the false memories the therapist had been implanting in their minds. So if Susan wanted more attention, Susan learned to tell her therapist about the sexual abuse with her father in great detail. Susan's stories became even more and more detailed.

Victims are often told before the memory is remembered; they might feel like it didn't happen. In fact, it might even feel like a dream and this was normal. But the victim is encouraged to push beyond those feelings and start talking about the abuse even if it felt like they were making it up. After all the memories had to come from somewhere, right? As I recalled Susan's story and as I was listening to Steve's story I couldn't help but think this therapy has to stop. How can a therapist do this to their patients? How can a family suffer destruction based upon memories of an event, which never happened? In the case of Marion Knox, why on earth was he allowed to continue for so long?

Steve and I began putting together the foundation of this book. I posted a few internet blogs regarding repressed memories and the teachings of Marion Knox. We began receiving "e-mails" from other families devastated by this type of therapy. One such anonymous story reads as follows and there are hundreds of stories told and reported in the same light across the country.

"From somewhere in Oregon,"- We lost our daughter through psychological counseling.

"We have lost our wonderful daughter through psychological counseling. Until two and a half years ago, my daughter, age twenty eight, and I were close. In fact, she was close to our whole family. She was an easy child to parent and she later worked diligently to earn her nursing degree. She went to a marriage and family therapist for counseling two and a half years ago. Our daughter had felt very depressed. She may have experienced burnout, or it may be some form of mental illness. She was depressed on and off during her teens, but not as badly. She was wrongly diagnosed. We think her therapist was over-zealous and induced memories our daughter had been sexually molested as a child.

Our daughter told me when she went to therapy the counselor told her right away, "I know just what's wrong with you. You were sexually molested as a child." Our daughter said, "Oh, no. I am sure I was not." After more 'therapy' from this woman, our daughter began believing it, and she thought it was so neat her therapist knew right from the start what was wrong with her. Our daughter said her therapist said, "It's usually done by the father in the family." She was trying to get our daughter to

269

"remember." She was beginning to have what she called "memories." I questioned my husband, and he said absolutely not. He had never ever sexually molested her or any of our children, I believed him completely.

The therapist took our girl to a private sex abuse clinic in "the big city." They believed her so-called "memories and carried on from there with therapy making her punch punching bags to get her hate out at her perpetrators. They developed an awful anger in her. She will not see us anymore.

The tragedy is none of these "memories" happened. Those aren't memories she's having. Then she began having "memories" we were cult members and devil worshipers and we cut up babies and sacrificed them. She is being driven out of her mind. Last Christmas I sent her some shoes and she cut them all up, carved into the soles and sent them home. She thought she had to do this to keep from getting a demon. She thought we were putting a curse on her. At Christmas, when we saw her, she had to have the therapist at her side who, after our daughter's accusations, kept telling us, "this is right, you did molest your daughter, and this is right, you did, you did, cut up those babies. You are just repressing it." We are Christians from many

270

generations back. We have never had anything to do with devil worship!

We wanted to go down there when our little girl was at the sex abuse center, but we were told it would be better if we did not. We were not included in therapy even though they claim to practice "family therapy." The therapist will not see us or answer our phone calls. We've tried for a year. If she is a family therapist, it seems she would include us. Our daughter is very suggestible, trusting, and believing. We feel she was talked into those things easily, at a time when she was already burned out and depressed. Those "memories" seem so real to our daughter, but we know for sure they aren't memories."

Steve told me this story is eerily familiar to his own. Steve's wife was taken advantage of when he claims she was very susceptible to persuasion because of her physical ailments at the time. We will explore this type of story and others who have given us permission to use their story for this book.

Lighting Strike by Mark Coldren

Chapter Fourteen
The Stories come rolling in as more victims come forward.
By Teila Tankersley and Stephan Skotko

We all think, " it can't happen to us, we would never fall for a therapist feeding us false memories." Yet, for the most part when we are at the point when we need to confide in a therapist we are usually at our weakest moments.

Individuals like Marion Knox who practices "repressed memory therapy" have been doing it for so long they have their method down pact. It's not only repressed memory therapy, but inner child therapy, Satanic Ritual abuse (SRA), and they reek of spiritual abuse. The men and women who Marion Knox victimized or attempted to victimize were all just ordinary people.

Here is a testimony from a gentleman who met Marion Knox back in the summer of 2003; while he was working with a man who maintained a small fleet of charter motor coaches. The two would meet daily for lunch at the local cafe and one morning his friend received a phone call from Marion Knox, who asked to join them for lunch.

"It started out harmless, we met up with Knox at the café, and this was my first meeting with Knox. Knox opened up immediately by sharing this theory he had about the "Free Masons". You see, Marion believed the Free Masons were abusing children, in the form of sodomy. The subsequent repressed memories from these children the Masons had abused resulted in some mental difficulties as these children got older," He stated.

273

"My friend didn't say much during the conversation. I offered little input, as I wasn't fully a part of the discussion. I was only present and if anything, it was just an interesting theory. A year later, my wife and I were having some marital problems. She had asked me to go see a counselor she had met, named Marion Knox. She had heard Knox was a Christian counselor who dabbled in repressed memory therapy. It was her hope Marion Knox could help our marriage. She was hoping Marion Knox could rid me of a "demon" she believed I was possessed by.

I never felt she had a balanced view when it came to spiritual issues. However, I felt compelled to do what I could to cooperate with her. My wife was simply upset because I no longer felt physically attracted to her and had no desire for intimacy. She was hoping Marion Knox could get to the root of things.

Regardless, I had tried to tell her my feelings and I explained to her it had nothing to do with "demons." She still thought Marion's counseling could "fix it." She refused to accept it was a medical issue many males have. Instead she began insisting it was "demons".

I met with Knox at his home in Lebanon, Oregon and explained the situation. He began asking me a few leading questions to find out what I thought about repressed memories. I told him I was neutral on the position. I neither felt pro or con about it. I wasn't educated enough on the subject to make an intelligent decision about it.

Knox then asked me if I had ever heard of the Masons or the Illuminati. I of course said, yes. At this point he excused himself from the small room we were in and within a few minutes, he returned to the room "wielding a huge sword and wearing a garb consisting of a scarlet cape, a funny looking hat, and an apron of sorts, which had some kind of fur or a 'mane' at the bottom."

I was both stunned and freaked out at the same time. I'd never experienced anything like this. I've seen some strange things but this was pretty out there. Here was a man I barely knew swinging a sword and acting out in a bazaar manner. I had no idea what this mad man was going to do to me with this sword! I was so concerned, I actually let out a cry; my mind couldn't comprehend the fear I was feeling, this was really crazy. All I could think of was I might be able to fend off a blow or two, but this man, in my opinion, has lost it! I believed I was in grave danger. I knew his behavior was just not right and downright bizarre!

Soon thereafter, Knox calmed down a bit, and I regained my composure. Knox had quit flinging his sword and he began asking if I had any relatives who were Masons. I had none, so I told him. Yet, Knox began trying to explain to me he believed based upon my reactions, I had been sodomized by someone in my family who was a Mason. He speculated it must have been my grandfather on my mother's side. He believed it had too of happened at a Masonic meeting.

When I returned home, my wife met me and anxiously asked how it went. In her words, she'd "fully expected me to be healed, and delivered from my demon." I wasn't and I told her so because I never had one to begin with. I also told her in my opinion Knox was a fraud and a religious nut case. This did not go over well with her. She was angry at my statement. It wasn't long after this episode, our marriage ended.

Although I didn't know Knox, this experience vexed me. I'd never had such an experience like this ever before. I actually found myself searching my memories, even asking relatives who knew my grandfather if he'd ever been a Mason. To my knowledge and to this very day, I know my Grandfather on my mother's side was never a Free Mason. I can honestly tell you he was a good man and he always treated me good. Now was I sexually abused as a child? Yes, I was in fact, on two different occasions by two different individuals; neither one was ever charged nor nothing was ever done to them in the way of prosecution. This was in the "dark ages" when things weren't spoken of.

Do I remember being abused as a child? Yes! Did I repress any memory of the times I was abused and did I block out those who had done this to me? Emphatically no! I had not blocked out those memories. I didn't remember, but I wish I could have been able not to. You see, I remember everything, which was said and done. I have however, through the Grace of my Lord Jesus Christ, forgiven both men in my heart. This was and is the redeeming factor for my personal freedom from it all and my being able to cope with the trauma caused by those two men. Simply put, it all is in the past. Forgotten? No, not at all….."

This sort of behavior would land most therapists and counselors on the unemployment line. One begins to wonder about the ethical standards an individual like this submits themselves to. This incident is not isolated and other practices by Knox are revealing themselves. When I spoke with Steve he shared some pretty shocking information.

Steve stated, "When I first met Marion and Doris Knox they seemed to be an average elderly couple. A then friend of mine suggested we meet as he had spent some time with Knox. My friend 'DC' was the person I spoke of earlier who eventually was kind enough to step in and steal my last bit of business from me.

At the time "DC" was a friend and it was actually he whom I confided in the night my wife called the authorities on me, the first night of my nightmare. We had often done work for each other. We weren't the best of friends, but we weren't enemies either. The first night of the happenings was the final night I spent in my home. I reflect back now and this thought still shakes me to my core.

One night I was in my house, which I labored in for over seven years to remodel and provide a place of peace and comfort for my family. The next day I was forced to leave and I would never ever be able to go back. Unless an event such as this happens to you (the reader, humanity); you can never fully realize what it feels like. I think the most overused term when dealing with hurt people is "I understand what you are feeling" or something to this effect.

Don't ever tell someone experiencing trauma you understand them unless you have walked in those shoes. You may think you are consoling them, but you're not. They see right through you. An individual can show compassion without saying things or lying to the victim. The victim does not need to be lied to. Just listen if you want to be a friend and help them.

I thought I would just interject this little piece of advice and bit of wisdom. My wife and I spent about 4 hours with the Knox's at our first meeting. Things seemed pretty well as he began to share with us how he "ministers" to people. "DC" had kind of explained a little to me.

Basically what Knox does is just ask questions. He asks you to just say the first word or impression, which comes to your mind. He says be honest and say what comes to your mind first, whether you believe it to be the truth or not.

In my situation he was really interested in the fact I was raised Catholic and especially in the fact I was an altar boy when growing up.

My situation and circumstances came up toward the end of the first night. It gave me something to think about for the next six months until we would see him again. For a while I felt better about myself. However, I did carry a bit of resentment from my childhood. We have all read

279

about and have experienced growing up. All of us have horror stories when we were children of being hurt or hurting others. My life was no different. There were a lot of individuals I despised from my childhood. I did not hate them. It is just I did not like them. Going to a Catholic high school presented its own set of unique circumstances in growing up, which I won't discuss at this time.

It would be almost six months before we would see Knox and his wife again. This second meeting or event transpired on New Year's Day 2004. It was after this meeting, in which I walked away fully realizing Marion Knox was a total nut job. He was and is way out in left field. In fact he is not even in the ball park; he resides out in the parking lot! The questioning took on a whole new meaning. This meeting consisted of my daughter, wife, the Knox's and me. Doris Knox was also present taking notes. We spent the whole day there. We ate lunch and dinner there this day. Out of this meeting came the following explanation of our problems by Knox.

It was Knox's belief my wife had been molested by her father as her mother watched. Knox convinced her she had had been forced to watch her father have sex with her sister while her mother coached them. Eventually my wife believed this. Then all of a sudden she began having memories and at one point claimed she could vaguely remember having a wet bath towel thrown over her head. She was two years old as she sat naked on her father's lap while he sodomized her. Later Knox would take her down the path of satanic ritual sacrifices of a human baby and convinced her at one point she drank the blood of a baby and ate its cooked flesh.

Knox went onto convince my daughter she had been molested by my step-son and his friends. She had been molested (sodomized) by my father the night before my father passed away. Then Knox had my daughter believing my wife's brother had anally sodomized her. Then she was sodomized by my mother with a crucifix.

Knox further convinced my daughter she was forced to drink her own blood mixed with wine at a ceremony conducted by a "special priest" and my father, supposable in the basement of our home.

Knox tried to convince me I had been anally sodomized as a child by of all people, my father as well as several catholic priests. He went on to say my mind had repressed those memories. He felt I was offered to the Catholic Church as a sacrifice to be a Jesuit priest since I was the first-born son. Knox also said my father followed this ritualistic approach for my life to restore our family name in the Catholic Church.

He suggested firmly asserted those priests had locked me in a box and closet for hours on end until I agreed to be sodomized, perform oral sex on the priests and participate in a "black mass."

Since Knox claimed I had been sodomized in his opinion, I was pretty much dammed and he of all people was only able to help me. The statement he made, which really shook me was, "if you are Catholic and especially an altar boy, then you have unmistakably been sodomized by a priest." There was no doubt in his mind. I had been!

He said I was living an evil life. He further stated because of every time, which transpired in my life I should be a homosexual instead of heterosexual.

I have always had times when I could not sleep throughout the night and I would get up sometimes at 2 or 3 in the morning. This he explained was the fact why I could not sleep next to my wife because my inner demon or urging was repulsed by the fact I was married, and I preferred men over women. So getting up and leaving the room was a subconscious reaction. It in fact confirmed I felt repulsed by my wife, which in reality couldn't be further from the truth. Later I would discover my wife believed all of this line of B.S. Marion was shoveling!

I would have left early in this second session because this guy was way off his rocker but my wife threatened me with the kids and leaving me if I did not get the "help" I needed.

This day totally screwed up our family and we never recovered as a family. My relationship with my daughter was never the same and at this point she began to get wild. She did not finish high School and started staying away from home for extended periods of time once she was 18. My daughter hung around till she was eighteen, but after she turned eighteen, it was a crazy life for her.

Every parent can attest to when a child turns the years into adulthood. You want to help them, yet you want them to be independent. You want to lay down the rules of the house, yet you don't want to treat them as a child. You want to begin respecting them as adults. It's not easy and one hopes their children will turn out better than themselves.

Knox made the following statements in the Affidavit of Arrest to detective Fairall. *"Marion told me he had developed the distinct impression Stephan was a "FLAKE" and totally*

283

untrustworthy. He told me he felt the wife would be truthful with me, (Marion seemed to be under the impression I had not yet talked with the Skotko family.) He told me he didn't know how much the Skotko children lie but daughter was "BACK AND FORTH." I asked him what he meant and he said daughter had left home and was taking drugs for a period of time. He described she would say she wanted to be a Christian and live a Christian life, and then she would go and hang out in a bar. He told me he had the same feelings about Stephan Skotko but wife was different. He said wife was a "CLASSIC VICTIM" of abuse. She said she seemed very depressed as to how her life had gone."

What I want to know is if this guy was not any sort of an educated counselor or therapist, why did the police believe him when he stated my wife was a classic example of a victim of abuse? How in the world does he know, how can he diagnose, and how can he make those assessments?

My daughter never had this type of described behavior until after she met Knox. My wife was prone to believe because she was suffering from the effects of her medical condition and Vitamin D deficiency. Knox never ever considered other factors. He just banged away on the sodomy and abuse band wagon. He never considered or encouraged other medical issues for the depression and other physical ailments. He just threw it in the "witch's pot of abuse." With Knox it is sodomy and abuse or the highway. He wants to hear no other and as others are attesting, they experienced the same with the same outcome.

Literally for the next three years I worked on trying to find medical help for my wife. In most cases she refused because she believed Knox's theory for her ailments. It was during these next 5 years, 2003 – 2008, which my wife and children would visit Marion Knox from time to time. During this time she began to estrange herself from the reality of life and friends. Later on during one of our court appearances she would always have someone with her.

For instance, she stated to me on more than one occasion she hated and despised our next-door neighbor Kaye. She wanted nothing to do with her. Kaye would stop over every once in a while to visit (Kaye was a bit nosey). My wife would always say you answer the door; I don't want to talk to the B----. When my DHS hearing came around, low and behold, who was in the courtroom? Why it was Kaye. I went over and talked to her and said to her, "why Kaye it's nice to see you" Kay replied, "Yes I am just here to give your wife moral support" How convenient was this?

Then there were our old neighbors from our previous residence in Albany, Tonya and Heather. Tonya and Heather is a same sex couple who lived across the street. Tonya had a son the same age as my oldest son. They went to high school together. My wife for the longest time would not permit my son to be friends with Tonya's son because of their lifestyle.

This never did bother me. In fact I did a lot of work in their home. Although my wife distanced our children from one another we continued to be social with Tonya and Heather after we left. Tonya and Heather are wonderful fantastic people. Both of them are social workers working with delinquent youth. They are good people. Once we moved into our new home I continued our friendship. In fact it was Tonya who came to our new house first and brought us a house warming gift. It was Tonya and Heather who hosted a super bowl party in 2008, which we attended.

My wife never did like them or trust them and wanted nothing to do with them. On more than one occasion I would come home to an earful how she thought Tonya had the "hots" for

286

her and made passes at her. This of course she said caused a lot of grief with Heather and on one occasion my wife contemplated filing a restraining order to stop Heather from "threatening" her.

When I went to my first appearance for my divorce hearing guess who was present? Yep, it was Tonya. In both of these cases she surrounded herself with people she hated and despised for "moral support."

To this day a lot of things mystify me. Was I being set up all these years by my wife? Was she doing this because of her mental state and not know fully what was going on? Was my wife crazy all these years? Was my wife brainwashed by Marion Knox? I have my suspicions, but I am still trying to figure a lot of things out.

Starry night

Chapter Fifteen
Bit by bit Unveiling Research Material for the
Book. By Teila Tankersley

"Second star to the right and straight on till morning." James T. Kirk

I really believe Steve had nothing to hide; in fact he even encouraged me to contact Kirk Johnson, Ph.D. a Licensed Psychologist and

288

Certified Sexual Offender Treatment Provider.

Dr. Johnson is the founder of the Vancouver Guidance Clinic P.S., providing a variety of forensic and clinical psychological services for over 25 years. His vision is to provide Clark County, Washington with expertise in the field of forensic psychology. This has led Dr. Johnson to specialties in the area of legal competency, criminal responsibility, child custody, and sexual offender evaluation and treatment.

Prior to receiving his Ph.D. from the University of Arizona and becoming a licensed psychologist, he was a juvenile probation officer in Lane County, Oregon. He has directed child and family programs, as well as outpatient and emergency services, at a community mental health center. He is a licensed psychologist in the state of Washington and also certified in the state as a Sex Offender Evaluation and Treatment Specialist. Steve was thoroughly examined by Dr. Johnson and was given a clean bill of health.

Provided with some of the court documents and leads from Steve, I began researching Steve's story to unravel more on this mystery. I wanted to know just who Marion Knox was and what he believed. To many in the community Marion was known as a farmer and a singer. He performs with his brothers in the Knox Brother Gospel Quartet. He is also a self-proclaimed family counselor.

Upon further research I was introduced to a few startling documents. The documents were two separate interviews of Marion Knox, one written by Elana Freeland, the other written by Ron Patton. These interviews reveal most of Marion Knox's beliefs; which we ascertain to be barbaric and bizarre. After reading through these I was convinced Marion Knox was "off his rocker."

The interview conducted and written by Elana Freeland portrays a picture of a man who is completely obsessed with the topic of sodomy. It became evident it was Knox's impression the majority of the sins in this world were the cause of sodomy alone. What was most startling was only after his repressed memory sessions was he able to convince the majority of his patients they'd been sodomized.

In Freeland's interview, Knox went on to say sodomy "attacks the nerves at the base of the spine and causes something neurological to happen within the brain. It also has a spiritual demonic component to it, which affects the person's mind in a way like nothing else will. In other words, I would state it this way; for a person to be able to develop multiple personalities they would have to be sodomized between the ages of two and four." The interview goes on to quote Knox as stating, sodomy was "the Egyptian initiation of the child to open the third eye." He went on to explain, "Sodomy changes the way the mind works; it opens the mind up to the spirit world."

If this isn't crazy in its self, he goes on to explain, "Females are best for becoming programmed computers or human recorders. Most women are more capable of creating multiple personality systems because of the way their minds work. But the fact is, men are more aggressive, so the percentage of women who are sodomized and become perpetrators is far lower than the percentage of men who become perpetrators. They're all victims to start with, but women just go on being victims, they don't tend to turn into perpetrators themselves.

I've worked with men who did not become perpetrators and remained victims, just like the women; and I've seen evidence of women who became perpetrators. Witches are perpetrators, and just like men, they're molesters.

I've worked with people who had women sodomizing them with objects and molesting children. But the percentage is lower with women than it is men.

A higher percentage of men will transition from victim to perpetrator. I'm convinced there are some men who compartmentalize in such a way they do not on the average remember acts of molesting; they will only remember if they get into this particular compartment. Otherwise, they have amnesiac barriers between the different compartments of their minds. Women are this way also.

A perpetrator with an amnesiac barrier is a sad case because they can switch into a certain compartment and go out and molest, then switch out and not remember. This is the kind of person they use in Special Forces for their assassination teams because they can activate the hidden compartment, which has been programmed for assassination and send them out on a mission.

A man who claimed to have been in the South African Special Forces told me of two cases where he was sent to assassinate, one in a national park in South Africa, and another in London."

It became obvious reading through some of these interviews Marion was really "out there". One would have to believe there would be a rebuttal or a disclaimer, which would follow these interviews in which Marion Knox would state he'd been misquoted or they were totally fabricated, however, this was never the case.

In the second interview written by Ron Patton titled, "THE MASTER PLAN OF THE ILLUMINATED ROTHSCHILDS". I was originally preparing to write up a short summary of these interviews but because I found them so unbelievable I decided it best to include this interview for you so you could see and read verbatim for yourself.

`*"Marion Knox is a farmer, Gospel singer, and counselor living in Lebanon, Oregon; for several years, he has been helping set people free from the affects of ritual abuse and mind control. Although some may think of his methodology as unorthodox, it appears to be effective in eliminating highly structured dissociation in many of the people he's worked with. While tediously assisting and supporting these survivors, Marion has uncovered startling information concerning the inner-workings of the Illuminati, the Rothschilds, and a possible end-times scenario. His conclusions are not only based upon what his clients are uniformly conveying, but also through Biblical and historical research. Mr. Knox would like to emphasize some of his opinions are speculation or conjecture and needs to be objectively verified and validated by independent sources with knowledge of the subject.*

Ron Patton: So when was it you started to first work with victims of SRA (Satanic Ritual Abuse), and mind control?

Marion Knox: to begin with, my first experience with anything dealing with the occult was through a friend of mine who thought his house was haunted. So I volunteered. While trying to figure out what was going on, a woman living in the house felt she was possessed. We went through a deliverance session with her and she eventually became a Christian. After this, I worked with people who had common sexual abuse. It wasn't until several years later in 1993that I started counseling on a regular basis those who were ritually abused. So as far as the satanic stuff goes, I first worked with three women who had multiple personalities, put in several hundred hours with each of these victims and as a result I began to understand the perpetrators belief system.

RP: So what did you basically learn about the perpetrators belief system and motives.

MK: since I already had a pretty good understanding of the Bible, it gave me part of the picture. But what I learned from other sources and what the survivors were telling me help put it together more clearly. Basically, Satan's system is built on the mirror image principle to copy the kingdom of God. The perpetrator's goal is to gain power. They believe the devil has the most power, and the most powerful component in the rituals is the blood sacrifices in blasphemy of Christ's atonement. Another very important component is the act of sodomy, which is the opposite of the "new birth" we have in Christ. The ritual abuse system is normally built around a three-year-old child, because this usually is the optimal time to create dissociation or MPD. This system is actually a mirror image or reflection of what appears to be a shattering of the core personality. To illustrate it better, let's say you stand between two mirrors and look down the corridor. You can then see yourself in multiple representations to infinity."

RP: Can you elaborate further on how the ritual abuse system is formed and how it works?
MK: Well, as I began to work with more survivors, I gathered more details and was able to kind of form a victim's profile. So as I

mentioned before, they take a child at approximately three years of age and make the child fast for several days, force the child to witness human sacrifices, and to participate in a cannibalistic communion service. In some instances, they physically abuse the child and then place him or her in a cage or coffin to further the trauma. The child is sometimes drowned in a baptismal ceremony and brought back to life. In the process of all this blasphemy, the child's mind is reversed or shattered into multiplicity. The act of sodomy is also performed to open up the victim's "third eye" which is supposed to enhance psychic ability. During this vial act, a demonic system called, "Legion" is installed. In the King James Bible, Legion is referred to as an, "unclean spirit". This is systematically done to have complete control over the child, like creating a programmed robot."

We have gathered testimonies of families devastated by Knox's teachings. One family shared the following information. Steve wanted to have this particular story here because it was so much what he had to endure with his own daughter and her involvement with Marion Knox.

*Dear Kathy, (written to a third party)-
LDS refers to Latter Day Saints or the Mormons.
Your card was like a breath of fresh air. Yes, we
have been wounded and devastated by the
counsel of Marion Knox who works continually
to turn our daughter against her family. We are
also angry such a screw ball is still lose out
there, going from church to church, preying on
women, labeling them with his generic stand of
being molested by family and or LDS persons at
age 3. He put our daughter under a trance of
some sort and brought out stories of many family
members abusing her when she was three years
old.*

*Knox also told her LDS persons rape and
kill babies in their temples. He was a little
frustrated when one of our sons explained to him
none of the family members he and our daughter
were accusing were Mormons! If Knox weren't
such a seriously sick person, it would have been
funny seeing him groping for words and his face
turning red, upon learning he had wrongly
assumed our extended family was all LDS.
Nothing seems to stop his egotistical absorption
with power and hatred of "Mormonism."*

(Steve can attest to this personally. He
stated to me the following; "on a later visit to

Knox's home for a Sunday morning bibles study I attended with my wife because I did not trust him. He made the same statements to me concerning the LDS temples having underground hidden chambers for their cannibalistic sacrifices and sodomy rituals of young child as initiation.

Well as we would have it at this same time they were constructing a new LDS temple in Albany Oregon. Being a contractor I became curious. I stopped one day and talk with the contractor. I asked him about such an accusation. He laughed and showed me the 3 feet of rock laid and compacted for the foundation. Then he explained to me the concrete slab foundation was going to be 12" thick with rebar enforcing.

If they were to have secret chambers it would be next to impossible to cut through this once it was poured. I watch this construction site from beginning to end. There was never anything put in the ground first to have such a chamber. When I told this to Knox at this bibles study, his faced turned red and he got angry at me. Shortly thereafter my wife called the police.)"

Knox is not the Christian he claims to be. He is hateful, self absorbed, tyrannical, egomaniacal man who feeds on vulnerable people who almost worship him. Without ever seeing me, let alone knowing me, he diagnosed me with multiple personalities. Later, when I met him, I told him to stop diagnosing someone whom he hadn't met and who hadn't turned to him for advice. The man is a lunatic of sorts. Underneath his "friendly" exterior, he is a control freak. His wife jumps to please him, and he doesn't like being questioned.

We know many people are abused in any number of ways. We support women's shelters and other effective sources of help for the abused. The reason we couldn't take our daughter's stories seriously was her stories were so obviously ridiculously untrue.

She accused a cousin and his wife of abusing her at a time when the cousin was not only unmarried but he had not even met his future wife at this point. She refused to confront them or others of her supposed abusers. She would socialize with them, and then at other times, for the purpose of keeping her stories going with her "friends,"(Knox, Rhonda Earle, et al) she would claim she couldn't go to a family affair because "so and so" would be there. None of the accused relatives ever babysat our children. When Jack trained at Ann Arbor, we came to Oregon once a year to visit, but from the beginning, when my sisters and I married, my

299

*parents by choice always made it clear they were
no "babysitting grandparents."*

*Our daughter also fabricated so-called
entries in a journal and dated them way back in
time. When she showed them to us, we noticed
they were written on Franklin Journal sheets,
which hadn't even been printed by the date she
claimed to have written the entries. (Franklin
journal sheets had their print date on them).*

*From time to time, she opened up.
Example, one day our daughter and I were on the
phone for an hour or so, and when she was going
on and on about something, I felt prompted to say
to her, "I've got time and I am listening carefully
to everything you are saying. But, I do want you
to know I know it is BS." She said "Mom, I'm
glad you are such a strong woman. You're right.
Even when I want to tell the truth, I have to work
so hard at each word to make the truth come out,
because otherwise, the lies just roll off of my
tongue." Another time she admitted she was the
best chameleon. Whatever group she was with,
from hippies to whomever, she outdid them all
and was the best at their trade. So apparently she
fits in with Knox and her present church group
by being the most abused.*

*With the combination of drugs and Knox,
our daughter was a very mixed up little girl. Over*

300

the years, our daughter became more and more pathological in her lying. We feel Knox was at the crux of this. He introduced her to a whole new area of fabricating. It was also when she was living with the Knox' (after they saved her from the streets of Eugene Oregon to save her from "the Mormons." she first became pregnant. Her stealing escalated to calling an elderly aunt from she was in Colorado with slashed tires and needed $400.00 to get new ones. She also tried to steal $1100.00 from an uncle and was involved in a bank robbing schemes cashing thousands of dollars of fraudulent checks with two guys. She was really in serious trouble when thank goodness; she got arrested for passing out in a car on the freeway shoulder with two babies in the car.

Well I have gone on and on, though I have barely scratched the surface. The good news is after spending six months in an in-house program for single mothers with children; our daughter is now nearly 18 months clean, dry and working so hard at being a good mother and person. She no longer steals and is working so hard to be honest. We are so proud of her. She is in Portland, and we either go up there or bring her down to Junction City. We all enjoy being with her and she likes being with family.

301

The down side is in the Knox circles; she continues to say what makes her an important part of Knox and his circle of vulnerable who kiss her feet. In some respects, I think she is confused enough (mentally/emotionally). She actually believes some of her/his own stories, having told them for over six years. Why else would she continue the association? Thus all is not right. Knox is still in her life. Knox also has some friends (people we knew well ago who have gone off the deep end) who have baptized her in their church and with Knox, manipulate and control her. As far as she has come and as hard as she has worked at the recovery, it is hard to believe she actually believes these people are friends.

Thank you for your good efforts. It is such a relief someone is organizing to stop Mr. Knox's psychological masquerade!

With much appreciation, ____*Junction City, Or.*

Golden Fireworks by Petr Kratochvil

Chapter Sixteen
Spiritual Abuse

"If our focus is placed upon the opportunity to get stronger as a result of our failure or misfortune instead of how weak we are because of our failure or misfortune, then there is no mountain we cannot conquer in life." Steve Skotko

It is a fact our lives as humans are directly influenced by our thoughts and emotions. It's part of what makes us humans and distinguishes us from animals. Some people are stronger in certain areas of life than others.

Inevitably you will discover individuals,

303

which are stronger physically than yourself, while others seem to have a certain degree of mental and emotional strength.

All of us have friends, acquaintances, and even enemies we admire for their inner strength. We have coworkers or we know someone who tells us of others who have exceeded expectations for themselves. We read magazine articles or watch the news and witness people who have beat the odds and conquered cancer and other diseases.

The opposite also holds true. Over the course of time you will no doubt have the opportunity to observe certain individuals who are weak in specific areas of their life. Often times this weakness has been caused by some kind of abuse, whether psychological abuse or in a Christian perspective, spiritual abuse.

The meat of my growing years was the 1970's. The 70s were rife with religious extremists taking advantage of people and forcing their beliefs on them. Jim Jones, Reverend Moon, the shepherding movement, and others taught and showed us the extreme side of spiritual and authoritarian abuse.

Spiritual Abuse occurs when a leader, belief system; whether religious or secular, or a church well intentioned or not, dominates, manipulates or castigates individuals through fear tactics, mind control, or some other psychological or emotional abuse.

Spiritual abuse just does not stop there. It can be inflicted in day to day life and by those we would never suspect. Spiritual abuse, I personally believe, is the worst level of abuse, which can be experienced by an individual.

When someone abuses you spiritually they are stripping you of your inner power and self-esteem. They are attacking your soul. They are inflicting huge hurt and trauma on your Core Value. This can happen no matter the religion. Catholic, Protestant, Hindu, Muslim, it does not matter.

Spiritual Abuse can be instigated by any form of religious authority. If religion is not involved it can be perpetrated by doctors, therapists and counselors. When we allow ourselves to continue to be a victim of this level of abuse we are, in effect, handing over our power to the abuser. It becomes easier to give into the lie than it does to fight back.

Spiritual abuse is about someone taking control over a person's mind, thoughts, creativity and dreams. These are the things, which motivate us in life and move us to strive toward good things for ourselves, our family, and environment.

Spiritual abuse is about power and control. It seeks to dominate you, to manipulate you, in the end it renders you incapable of making your own decisions. It opens the door to all other abuse including physical abuse, sexual abuse and spousal abuse.

If someone can destroy your spirit, then you become mentally paralyzed. You are unable to reason your decisions and thought processes. You begin to see and feel things, which are not there. "You begin to ignore the fact the abuse is undeserved treatment; therefore, depleting your self-esteem." [3]

Low self esteem keeps us locked into unhealthy or toxic relationships with others. When we continue to allow ourselves to become spiritually abused, it is only a matter of time before this abuse becomes physical.

Painful relationships whether professional or intimate develop for many reasons. Sadly, there are times when people hurt people out of meanness; they intentionally use, abuse, and damage the other person.

At the same time, many harmful, toxic interactions have nothing to do with the desire to cause pain. The troubles may be largely due to a person's own emotional wounding, stressful lifestyle, mental illness or addiction to alcohol and other drugs.

Spiritual abuse is the most challenging form of abuse to heal from. The wounds from physical abuse will heal in time but healing from spiritual abuse takes tremendous effort on the part of the survivor to overcome. The survivor must completely reprogram his or her thinking in order to build a new self worth and inner strength, which will prevent them from ever becoming a victim to spiritual abuse again.

I was amazed when people started to tell their stories after the first newspaper article was written. Amazed perhaps is not the proper word. I really was not amazed other families began telling their stories. I was more stunned to the similarities we all experienced them. So far, most of the stories surround themselves by parents and the effects of this counseling on their children or other family members.

To this point I have not met another person who was forced to endure the same sort of thing as myself. The closest one would be Mr. McCracken in 2002. I have not had the opportunity yet to meet him personally or correspond with him in any sort of fashion.

Sadly, the mask of spiritual abuse deception can be worn by anyone. Including but not limited to spiritual systems, churches, both unbiblical and biblical, authority structures, and of course cults. Even the philosophy and ideology of large and small corporations can inflict spiritual or psychological abuse on individuals. Doctors, therapists and counselors can also be perpetrators of spiritual abuse and psychological abuse.

All forms of spiritual abuse inevitably lead back to the one who is the abuser; and most often it is the leader of the group. Authoritarian abuse can simply be defined as a misuse and over emphasis on authority. An individual can be spiritually abused by their employers or bosses. "If they strip you of your self-worth, make you feel inadequate in your position, belittle or berate you, then you are suffering from spiritual abuse." Whatever an employer's intentions are if you begin to feel belittled, you are beginning to feel the effects of abuse.

For example, I recently was volunteering at a corporation. My time was donated for administrative purposes. I was happy and satisfied to freely give my one day a week with no pay in order to benefit myself, gain experience, and better the organization. They utilized my computer and writing skills. I worked in human resources and revamped most of their filing systems. It was a total mess. I am a bit anal when it comes to organization and was told and I felt as if I were contributing to the organization.

After several months I began to feel uncomfortable by the person in authority over me. For a time I simply wrote off those inappropriate feelings as to affects of my current personal situation.

As I worked there it was a natural flow to be acquainted with the regular personnel. I began to do repairs on things; filing cabinets and other little things, which needed to be repaired. My supervisors really used this opportunity to effectively apply the Hawthorne effect on the employees; this meant placing me on tasks, which let the employees know they were being observed, this would motivate them to do better and be more efficient. This is the Hawthorne effect.

Then the day came when I was asked to move furniture. This was not so much as an issue, as it was moving an office of an employee who had been sick for a number of weeks and was forced to take leave because the virus the individual was suffering from, a contagious virus I might add, was not going away. I felt the uneasiness, especially when I was promised a little bit of compensation by way of a gift card in order to do this task.

I never went back to this volunteer position. I never received the promised compensation either. I just was not ready to go there again and deal with the psychological aspects of it, so I did not. Spiritual abuse is just not suffered by religious systems. Spiritual abuse happens if your self-worth is threatened, weakened, or berated.

Other abusive systems, which are religious in nature claim they are 'led by God' and therefore justify their 'abusive behavior' by saying they are 'God's leaders', etc. Abusive leaders damage people in countless ways.

Recovering from spiritual abuse is a very painful process. Most people, who have never been abused spiritually or physically, etc., do not understand what recovering from spiritual abuse is like; and sadly, most people assume once a person leaves an abusive system, group, leader, or workplace the problem is over.

My time of separation from my family, however painful it is, has helped me to heal from the abusive power, which was in my home by way of Marion Knox. I was so involved in my life and helping my family, I did not even realize the root culprit was Knox. I remember feeling such an opposition in my life, and an uncomfortable uneasiness.

During this time I was on a short trip with a friend who was suffering from a handicap. I traveled with him because he needed an aid to help him. I spoke with him about my feelings and we could not figure out what the problem may have been. I know one thing, when I was away from home during this time, I felt better. When I returned home from this trip the feelings resurfaced.

It was a short time later the accusations started from my wife and daughter. Also at this time, my wife had not undergone her surgeries or diagnosis yet. I assumed I was feeling the effects of the emotional strain from my wife as I knew she was suffering in her condition. I believe now with time I have been able to realize the amount of interference Knox had in my home.

When in the heat of the battle, it was unknown to me the cause; it was performed with stealth by my wife and Knox. I truly believe my wife was not even aware or still is not aware of what was really happening in our home at this time.

Her condition was being fed by the outlandish beliefs of this man posing as a kind Christian counselor. In many cases the suffering increases, as was the case with my wife. The more I fought for them all, the more they became prey to his teaching. Although a person may be free from the 'outside influence', the person now has to come to grips with their own crushed personality.

This is a good explanation of me. I was directly influenced by Knox. My personality as father and husband were crushed. The self esteem, which came from being father and husband, was slowly eroding away. Once I pulled away from the domination initially put on me by Knox, the effects of his authoritarian abuse still affected me by way of my wife and children.

Furthermore, in recovering from this spiritual abuse, the emotional trauma, mental scaring, and painful memories, which I have struggled with, I realize it can take many more years to go away. I do not think the effects and memories will ever go away completely. How can they, I still love them and will love them forever.

This is because of the way we are created. Holding to my Christian standard, we are instructed to forgive. It never does command us to forget. I believe it is because we never can. The basis for the counseling methods used by individuals like Knox is "we repress memories."

Also, the abuse he leads others to believe

happened to them at the hands of family is never given counsel to 'forgive.' I do not believe we as humans ever do forget anything. Memories are stored in our subconscious. Psychology states this is the way we were created. However, as I have determined for myself, It is those memories I want to use to get stronger and to hopefully encourage others to get stronger.

I believe every setback in life can be conquered in this way. Those who abuse drugs and alcohol are taught they will always be this way when they seek help through abuse programs. I believe we can change. I believe we can be free and the effects will no longer seek to control our heart, mind, and soul. If our focus is placed upon the opportunity to get stronger as a result of our failure and weakness instead of how weak we are because of our failure or misfortune, then there is no mountain we cannot conquer in life.

I empathize with those who are suffering and trying to become free from spiritual abusers. It is my whole reason and motivation for writing this book. It is my hope my recovering from spiritual abuse can be of help to any and all who are reading this.

These are the patterns I found in some of the families we spoke with as in the case of the

Junction City, Oregon family. They witness their daughter making gains yet are still puzzled with the magnetism within their daughter to the authoritarian figure their daughter has identified herself with. In this case it was Marion Knox.

The Bible, once misinterpreted, quickly becomes the most abused book in the world. Scripture abuse includes inaccurate quotations, twisted translations, ignoring the immediate context of Scripture, and reading into a text what is not there. These abuses (perversions) of Scripture or other religious text form the vast and subtle religious text twisting justifications of spiritual abusers.

It is the basis for the terrorism in our world. It is true the abuse of Scripture and other religious text is the foundation of an abusers deceit. Don't be fooled by those who would supplant [to supersede (another) especially by force or treachery] your eternity through Scripture or other religious text abuse. [1]

This claim is the crux of what Knox teaches and believes. From the Ron Patton interview we again quote Knox, *"Since I already had a pretty good understanding of the Bible, it gave me part of the picture. But what I learned from other sources and what the survivors were telling me help put it together more clearly.*

314

Basically, Satan's system is built on the mirror image principle to copy the kingdom of God. The perpetrator's goal is to gain power. They believe the devil has the most power, and the most powerful component in the rituals is the blood sacrifices in blasphemy of Christ's atonement. Another very important component is the act of sodomy which is the opposite of the "new birth" we have in Christ. The ritual abuse system is normally built around a three year old child, because this usually is the optimal time to create dissociation or MPD. This system is actually a mirror image or reflection of what appears to be a shattering of the core personality. To illustrate it better, let's say you stand between two mirrors and look down the corridor. You can then see yourself in multiple

Knox begins with the bible and then states other sources, but he never says what those sources are. He bases his therapy not on scripture, but on the other sources and survivors. What survivors? Where are they, who are they? If they were this important, one would think they would be mentioned. I believe those sources are Knox' own latent maniacal tendencies giving birth to perversion!

Looking from the outside, it can be difficult to fully understand the severity of the psychological abuse and how deeply it affects us as individuals. In my life men like Knox had their effects on me. But the most damaging and hurtful experience I had was watching and listening as my own family tried to speak and wield the lies supplanted in their minds by Knox. Even if you are experienced and trained in dealing with these kinds of situations, the answers can still be confusing and puzzling as to the ramifications of these social problems.

Many times people receive psychological abuse from their very own family members; in my case I feel as if the psychological abuse started when I became separated from my family at their own hand. When this is the case, often, the victim feels as though they have no choice and no option. I felt totally helpless in dealing with my own family members.

Numbness creeps into your mind, heart and soul. It is as if all your strength is drained in just keeping your sanity and combating the ideologies of men like Knox. Instead I began to feel trapped by my circumstances. When this happened I began experiencing the psychological abuse stemming from Knox and felt as though I had no way to prevent this kind of behavior on my part and was left without an adequate defense.

316

Shannon Cook lists these 6 signs if you have been psychologically abused, whether male or female.

1. You are put down verbally, in public and or private. These putdowns may be blatant or more subtle, but they all add up to make you feel worthless, inferior, or immoral. The individual uses this technique to make you feel powerless and dependant, and create the illusion they are superior.

2. An individual withholds or demands physical intimacy. (Intimacy is not limited to sex) If your partner denies you intimacy deliberately or demands you fulfill their desires, regardless of your state of being, this is an emotionally abusive tactic. Both the denial and the demand hold's you hostage and communicates to you your wishes and needs are irrelevant and not as important as the abuser's wants and needs.

3. There is an attempt on the individual's part to control your activities. If the individual demands an account of your daily activities, or puts pressure on you to only do certain "approved" things, this is a sign you are being emotionally abused.

317

4. An individual limits or attempts to limit your contact with family and friends. Isolation is a powerful technique for an abuser because it prevents you from getting outside perspective on what is going on in your life. If this individual gets upset or angry when you spend time with others, this indicates an abusive situation.

5. The individual implies non-physical punishment or threats if you do not comply with their demands and desires. Conversely, the individual may occasionally offer a kindness as a reward to keep you invested in the possibility your relationship with them can improve and can change.

6. You feel crazy, inferior, less intelligent, or question reality because of the things the individual says about you. For an abuser, keeping you off balance and feeling depressed and worthless ensures you will continue to feel dependent and under their control. [4]

Shannon Cook is a personal growth and relationship expert who has written a number of informative articles and e-books on the topic of toxic relationships and holistic personal growth, including physical, emotional and relationship health.

Time does heal most wounds. The first step is realizing you are suffering from or being abused spiritually or psychologically. Once you realize this you must decide to be free from it or it will take you down a long hill of devastation and shipwreck. You must recognize the perpetrator for who he or she is.

I received an email from a dear lady in Albany, Oregon. At first she stated she saw the newspaper article and was seeking emotional support. Her original email went like this.

"I'm referring to the article in the Albany Democrat Herald about Steven Skotko.
I live in Albany, Oregon with my husband and four kids. I've struggled with depression and an anxiety disorder all my life but anxiety gripped me worse than ever after a 5.5 earthquake woke me on a March morning in 1993; the same April I saw Marion for the first time. He was still at the infant stages of his ritual abuse concepts so he spent a good deal of time "investigating" with me but I always felt worse after seeing him. I was having extremely grotesque nightmares and what I thought were flashbacks but nothing made any sense. After seven years I learned I could not be healed by him as long as I referred or thought of

him as my god. [Later I learned I had postpartum psychosis.] I'm barely scratching the surface here. Trust me when I say it was brutal and hellacious. I've been seeing a licensed clinical psychologist for the last four years and only within the last few years have I finally realized how devastating Marion's influence on me has been.

I'm definitely interested in talking with others who have been through the Marion horrors. My husband and I have been alone for so many years we thought we were the only ones and everyone else had "healing" success stories. We wondered what was wrong with us."

I responded back with the following,

Regarding this email you sent me, do you still feel Marion was not wrong? This was the email I wanted to put into my notes for future use. Would you care to expand on anything about this?

Her final response was this,

You asked if I wanted to clarify or expound on anything. Please note, although it is your prerogative to bring civil action against Marion and Doris this is not my intent and I do not wish to be a part of it. As far as whether Marion was wrong I will say, yes, I do believe he was wrong in my case but sincerely so. I believe he doesn't hold any maliciousness and is not out to purposely hurt people. He truly believes in what he is doing and will see your lawsuit as a form of persecution, which will only serve to strengthen his resolve. My initial reason for contacting you, Steve, was for emotional support from other first-hand victims and this still stands.

If you fail to recognize the perpetrator for who he is you will never begin to get free from the hold he, she or it will have upon your life. If your views differ from those who you attempt to receive emotional support from, how do you think or believe the source will be able to help you. They never will.

The first step to healing is recognizing the perpetrator, admitting what they did to you, and then decide you are going to do all in your power to recover and better your life. This is the case of this poor woman. I cannot provide to her the support she seeks if our recognition of the problem differs.

This is how I have been able to get help and support. This is how all will get the help and support they seek. What does it matter if you think someone "purposefully or not" conducted themselves in a manner, which was or is inappropriate?

This is not the concern. The concern is they continue even when the outcomes are all the same. It is not just one issue or two. It is twenty and thirty years of this behavior and counseling. He keeps going and going with it.

A person can be walking down the street and accidently hit someone, this kind of action you can forgive and let go. But if a person walks down the street everyday and strikes people then you have a pattern. You must bring a stop to the pattern, which is proving to be destructive to others who are walking down the street.

Notes chapter 16

[1] http://www.spiritual-research-network.com/spiritualabuse.html. Retrieved January 12, 2011

[2] http://www.whale.to/b/knox.html. Retrieved January 14, 2011

[3] Kovabis Jones, 2010 Retrieved January 14, 2011 from http://www.helium.com

[4] http://EzineArticles.com/?expert= Shannon_E_Cook

Forest in the Fog by Giovanni Neri

Chapter Seventeen

From a man to other men, (no offense ladies)

"Have a heart, which never hardens, a temper, which never tires, and a touch, which never hurts." Charles Dickens

When the walls came crashing down in my life I know for a fact and believe with my whole heart I went into absolute emotional shock. Actually, what just happened to me, I did not know, I realized I was hurt and had no idea what to do next. Some of the best advice I received near the beginning came from my attorney, which was "baby steps, one day at a time."

Literally life was day to day and at times it was even hour to hour. This whole concept was something, which was going to have to permeate my being. This mentality had never been a part of my personality, ever. I had always acted on things and made things happen. I believe a lot of this had to do with my job. Being a self-employed general contractor had its benefits but also had its setbacks. When there was no work I never waited around for it to come to me. I had to "beat the pavement" and find work or somehow create work. The new mentality of "one day at a time" would drive me crazy, but now it is getting better.

Over the years of my life I remember hearing and reading stories of faith by individuals. I read of People who experienced miracles or other supernatural events; stories of missionaries and groups of people who were persecuted to the point of death and how their faith created resilience in them to survive. I never really could understand how a person or a group of people could "live by faith." Two and a half years later, I cannot even fathom living without faith. So many things have transpired along my journey. This has caused me to know God is fully and completely directing my footsteps along this path.

What a dramatic change has taken place in my life and to my thought processes. For this I am grateful beyond words. God has been good to me throughout my whole ordeal. I have been brought into new relationships with wonderful people, which I have met along the way. I never would have had my life enriched by them had I not suffered through what I did. Enrolling in school was so vital for me, as it kept my mind focused on other things and at the same time helped me stretch my mind. It has put me into contact with wonderful professional people, which have helped reshape my life. This has aided me tremendously in my healing process.

Every day brings something new to my life. I look at my healing process as an opportunity to fulfill my dreams and attain goals I set for myself years ago. Even before I was married these dreams and goals for whatever reason were placed on a side burner or back shelf in my life. "I want to thank you God for demonstrating so many things to me and in my life; for keeping my heart from turning hard and indifferent, and for your faithfulness in my darkest moments."

All the things Teila and I have mentioned in previous chapters regarding support and general information are in heavy volumes for women. Books upon books have been written for women by women; women who have been abused in one fashion or another. I wish we all could live in a world, which is free from abuse and abusive behavior. All of this information is good material and much needed in our society.

I have been hard pressed to find information written for men by men. My desire is for this chapter to be geared to men and for men.

My best friend Gale has been a constant encouragement to me. He kept telling me the same thing. "Hey bra, there are a lot of books out there written for women by women but there are none written for men by men." There are a lot of men who have been falsely accused in society and are in jail or prison for crimes they did not commit. There are a lot of men who have had to endure a tremendous about of legal mumbo-jumbo because they were simply men.

I know there are a lot of hurting men out there and hopefully this book may find its way into their hands. What became real apparent to me very quickly was how corrupt government can be. I know there are pockets of honest government processes, which exist, but for the most part "the system" is broke. It is nearly impossible to fairly investigate every accusation, which is made regarding abuse.

When I was victorious in my DHS hearing my attorney told me I won because I was right. I won because I was good people. I remember asking him along the way during the hearing if it was as apparent to him as it was to me the other side was not adequately prepared for the hearing. He told me "it's true Steve because normally guys in your position never fight this far, 99% usually give up, go away and just pay the support and never fight for their rights."

Does this make them all guilty, of course not? On the other hand it does not make them all innocent either. "They don't know what to do with you," my attorney stated. This is why my wife's and son's state appointed attorneys were inept in the cross examination, because I fought back.

What a waste of government money. I was unimpressed by their attorneys and their convictions on how to try and prosecute me during the hearing. This type of attorney is used to winning without a fight by the accused. They collect their government checks and then simply move on to the next case. I call them "CATFISH-Attorneys" they are scavengers and "bottom feeders." They exist to clean up the judicial system waste, which gathers at the bottom of the tank. These types of cases are always slanted against men!

As a man, being accused of sexually based crimes places a stigma on you. You are never presumed innocent until proven guilty. In the eyes of the DHS system you are forever guilty; if successful, you are just the one who "got away with it." I fought so hard because I did not want my name on any offender list for things I never did. In most states, in my opinion, the departments of family services consist of a lot of frustrated "individuals." Most of them victims of abuse themselves.

State governments favorably employ these single individuals to fill these positions. I am unsure yet as to why state governments do favorably employ this type of person so much. Most of these individuals have vendettas against men from the start, in their eyes you are guilty upon accusation and then forced to endure the limping legal process to prove your innocence. In total my defense and the process of being proven innocent cost me well over $500,000.00, when I take into account all the assets I lost along the way. This process bankrupted me and my wife defied the law and sold all my business assets and our joint possessions, or hid all of them in a neutral place. These acts were clearly against the law.

329

I am sure my wife felt justified in everything she did and probably had others who encouraged her and backed up all of her decisions. Nothing was ever liquidated as required by law, and the proceeds split. They let her take everything; furniture, appliances, electronics, family pictures, collectables and all knick knacks. I have not been able to determine as of yet to what all transpired after I was forced to leave my home.

I probably never will find out what really happened and this is all right by me. I am only stating it as it happened and the way, which it happened. I am not bitter at the system at all. There are two who know what really happened to all the possessions in my house, my wife and God. God keeps real good books and one day the truth will be made known!

I know and realize there are a lot of "pervs" out there; men who have done despicable deeds to women and innocent children over and over. There are also a lot of men out there who have done horrible things over the years who have never been caught. I believe as horrendous as things are and the atrocious things many have gotten away with, in time they will get theirs and receive their just reward, whether in this life or the next.

This does not bring a lot of comfort to the ones who have been abused by these monsters." Like I stated earlier in this book "life is not fair," but, we all have the opportunity to act upon our circumstances and improve ourselves. One could only hope at the least the scales of justice should be balanced so the innocent men don't suffer because of the real jerks and buttheads in the world.

When I was first asked by the detective on the telephone to meet him he used the term "domestic violence." The term domestic violence these days has a broad meaning and can be construed in many ways. When I met him he informed me it was not domestic violence but they wanted to talk to me about allegations I molested my children.

The detective stood there in the parking lot and told me he lied to me on the telephone so I would not flee. In fact when the original restraining order was filed against me and I collected my personal things, my passport was missing. I received it back months later in recovered business files. From the beginning they thought I would flee. I believe this because they were confident I was guilty of the allegations.

No one in government was ever honest with me and they always presumed as to what I would do. I never did any of it. In their eyes I was already guilty. In the police affidavit the detective stated I refused to answer questions and he thought this seemed funny and strange to him because I did not know what he wanted to question me about. I did know, and I knew who was really instigating this. He lied to me and he lied on the police affidavit. Detective Fairall of the Albany, Oregon Police department, "I submit you are a liar!"

Men remember this first thing. The police will lie to you and play on your emotional state. Mark it down, they will lie to you. The authorities always take the side of the party who calls first. I was told by my attorney to refuse the questioning and as my attorney stated later to me, "you were in an emotional state to not adhere to sound questioning. They would have twisted it around and got you to admit to things you never did." The police will lie, and they will always deny it or make it look like they never say anything especially when the conversation is not being recorded!

Second thing men, listen to your attorney. Period, listen to them and heed their counsel. When faced with the accusations my best defense was to say nothing. Once you start talking, then you get angry and emotional, and then you say things at a later time regret you have ever said. This is good sound advice to a lot of things in life."Keep your mouth shut."

At my hearing my attorney said "Steve don't show any emotion, just sit there and take it. Stone face dude, I want you to have a stone face, don't let anything, which is said in court arouse an emotional response. No smirks, no rolling of the eyes, just stone faced, you may think the judge is not watching but she will be. Stone faced dude, I want you stone faced. When you answer the questions on the stand, look at the judge. If you look at the judge when answering questions it will bode well for you."

Later on I thought about the reactions of others during the hearing. My wife and children could not look at the judge when answering the questions. Even Knox could not look at the judge and often tried to side step the issue and question at hand. In fact they all looked down at their feet. This meant they were not answering honestly or they did not believe what they were really saying was the truth. Even the district attorney would not speak loud. He was really quiet and low voiced.

On a number of occasions the judge had to ask him to speak up because the microphone was not picking up his voice. He could not speak up because he had no convictions in his heart I was guilty of what they were claiming.

Come on man, if you are going to try and prosecute me at least put meaning into it. If you are going to put me through the meat grinder at least show some feelings to it. Men listen to your attorney, period and do as they say!

Third, men fight for what you believe is right and never ever beg someone to like you or love you! If you have problems, fix them. I had to make some very hard, some very difficult decisions early on. I realized my family with the counseling of Knox wanted nothing to do with me any longer. This thought and the reality of this situation crushed me. It was like someone ripped my heart out of my chest, threw it on the ground, and just stomped on it. They wanted a life without me, my wife wanted out of the marriage. So I gave it to them and walked away.

I cannot tell anybody else to do this. Those are decisions you as an individual can only make for yourselves. There was no way I was going to force my will on anybody. In fact this was part of their beliefs coming through Knox; I was forcing my will upon them for a number of years. I always wanted my wife and children to be independent and I wanted them to make their own choices for their lives. My wife made the

334

decision to stay home and raise the children and for a time home school them. In turn in letting those make the decisions they wanted to make for themselves and when things did not work out for them; I was not going to step up and rescue them. Nobody did this for me and I wanted them to live with their decisions, and still do. This is the way we all learn.

You learn really quickly when you are a child if you touch the hot stove you will get burned and it hurts. But you learn not to touch it again! About three weeks before my wife turned the gas up in my life and called the police, she walked up behind me as I sat at my desk in my office. In a low quiet voice she said to me. "You really enjoy your work don't you?" Yes I replied. She then said, "I know no matter what happens you will always be a success and you will always do well."

I never would of believed you if you told me my wife was going to do the things she did and pit and turn my children against me. This statement about me always going to do well coming from a person who was plotting against me. I was to discover later; she was planning on destroying me, locking me up and throwing away the key. How diabolical is this and all along sleeping with me and telling me how much she

335

loved and appreciated me. Talk about psychological abuse!

Domestic violence is a term a lot of people associate as a man doing to a woman. Men suffer domestic violence maybe as much as woman, yet it goes untouched and unnoticed. Most men don't complain for whatever reason, just like it is impressed upon you as a man crying is a character weakness.

So what is domestic violence against men and how is it different from domestic violence against women? There are a number of definitions of domestic violence, none of which have been adopted universally to provide clear cut parameters to be used by researchers, governments and authorities. Like I stated, there is a general trend to define domestic violence in gender-specific terms, describing it as an act against women by men. Most definitions include physical, mental and emotional abuse, which affects the victim's well-being at home and in public life. I will support you men to the best of my ability if you are suffering from abuse, at least as long as you are innocent from displaying violence

Physical abuse includes the use of abuse such as slapping, punching, kicking, and biting; the use of weapons and sexual abuse. Mental or non-physical abuse includes psychological, emotional, verbal, spiritual and economic oppression. Although the common perception is men are unlikely to suffer serious physical damage from a woman, statistics and surveys reveal men are more likely to present for emergency treatment for more severe wounds than women. At the more subdued end of the spectrum, women will throw objects, punch, push, slap, bite and kick. They are also more likely to use a weapon, in particular knives and baseball bats to physically assault their partner.

Men tend not to recognize emotional and verbal abuse although if pushed will reveal these are probably some of the women's strongest tactics. Verbal abuse can include cruel and demeaning remarks designed to destroy a man's confidence in him. This is a very effective tool. A story came out in 1999 from Australia when a New South Wales magistrate claimed women provoked domestic violence by "bitching and nagging and emotionally hurting men," Australia's governments and feminist lobby were quick to condemn him. However, all government literature designed to educate women on the issue of domestic violence includes verbal abuse and describe all these things.

Men are also unlikely to report

psychological abuse; however, when pressed they say it is the most common form of abuse used by women. It includes public humiliation, making jokes at his expense and using threats, such as refusing access to children to maintain control of the relationship. Threatening to leave with the children and making his life hell, and lying to government in order to obtain a restraining order. It is also rare for a man to admit he has been emotionally abused. Men are more likely to report injuries inflicted with a weapon. However, emotional abuse can be one of the most dangerous weapons used by a woman and can include neglect, intimidation and the threat he will not see his children if he leaves or tells anyone what she does. Deprivation of loving feelings and closeness also constitute emotional abuse.

These were tactics used by my wife while she was receiving counsel from Knox during the time I was unaware of her receiving counsel from him. It also continues to this day. It continued after the criminal charges were dropped. The State of Oregon DHS by way of a Susan Juster continued to push the issues and deny me my legal rights to communication with my children even though there was no proof and there was proof they were being manipulated and they were lying about the molestations.

Now the legal quarreling is over and I should be allowed visitation in some sort or telephone communication, my wife is gone and the child support checks sit in her post office box not cashed. My son has not seen or spoken to me in all most three years. All he has heard is his mother's side of the story and I believe she has been brain washed by some psycho. Everything is still slanted against me without any foundation or substance because the State can do it. It is of no they can send me letters stating my son does not want to talk with me or see me. Why should he want to after being led into a room at school and having to endure questions from the police and social workers about how evil his dad is. This is all he has heard for almost three years.

When does it stop? It can cost another half million dollars for me to fight the system for my rights, which were taken away for no other reason except I was a man and was accused of things I did not do. So my question is this, who is really abusing my son? You may think you can control and manipulate circumstances to your benefit, but be it known your sins will find you out.

Finally, as I bring to close these thoughts I want to encourage men whom have suffered abuse and have been accused falsely. You are in control of your future no matter the circumstances. Whatever trial besets your life you are ultimately in control of you. You have the power to make a difference. You have the power to change. You may not want to think this, but you do have the power. We can control nobody except you

Because of my circumstances and what has been placed into my lap, the world is forever changed. There are men out there who think they may be getting away with some sort of abuse. Due to my circumstances I have written this book. Someone being abused out there in this world, by you the abuser, will find these words, take them to heart and decide to do something about their situation concerning you the abuser. Ultimately you will be found out.

If you are being abused, find help at once! Find a good therapist, get a good attorney, or confide in a friend. Do something about your situation. I decided to better myself not in order to write a book and profit, but I knew if I did nothing the perpetrators in my life and those who inflicted abuse and control into the lives of my loved ones and children would do it again. I knew if I did nothing someone else would get hurt. Another man would lose his home and family due to false accusations.

I know I have only scratched the surface, but I wanted to begin to make a difference and cry out for change to our system. It is broke as it is. Unless we all step up and speak out, nothing will change. I never want to ever be walking in a bookstore or a library and find a book like mine. I want to read about strong healthy families free from abuse. With an attitude such as this, we together can make a difference. I would encourage you to join our team. Involve yourself, reach out to someone who is hurting and has been a victim. See them healed and their minds restored. Be a part of seeing families wholesome and filled with love.

Enhanced Rainbow by Barb Ver Sluis

Chapter Eighteen
Searching for a Therapist?
By Teila Tankersley

In exposing the tactics of Marion Knox and the theory on "RMT" I became concerned this information might cause some individuals, out of fear, to avoid going to a therapist in the future. So along the way I sought out the advice from a few experts. I wanted to find out what exactly one should look for when searching for a therapist. I wanted to know what to avoid and how to spot the warning signs if your therapist is leading you astray.

Along the way, I've learned it is possible to find a good therapist and still practice caution. In fact I still believe seeking out a counselor; therapist, or psychologist is wise.

There are times in our lives we are in need of good counsel and we should seek out the assistance and expertise of a good and credible counselor. So, I do not want stories like Steve's to discourage any one from seeking guidance from a therapist. This chapter offers some tips and advice when looking for a therapist.

Deborah Reeves, MGPGP, LPC, CGP states, "Finding the best trained therapist is an excellent investment in one's future. Effective psychotherapy can help resolve conflict(s) and can greatly assist in helping all people to gain the emotional and cognitive tools necessary to better solve future problems."

There are times when a therapist is just what you need so never hesitate in confiding in one. Remember though, therapy is not magic, a therapist is not there to solve all your problems and they are not there to make decisions for you. If you think counselors and therapists are all the same, than think again. Usually by the time you are ready to seek the advice or counsel of a therapist you are at your wits end. So, before you make phone calls, here are some suggestions on how to proceed and what to look for. I decided to do some research in order to provide a layman's guide to choosing a therapist.

With the assistance of several well-respected counselors, therapists and psychologists I've bundled some great information together I think is beneficial.

David A. Reinstein, LCSW who is a clinical social worker psychotherapist, a mental wellness coach, staff trainer, and parenting educator offered some expert advice on this topic. David has been a therapist, trainer, and supervisor of therapists for many years, so he's come to understand the 'fit' between the client and therapist is essential to any successful treatment. He says "it is important there is a mutual respect and you as the client have a clear understanding of the nature of therapy, how it works, and what is required of each participant."

David has written many articles. In one he particularly points out some suggestions on what to look for when searching for a therapist.

You might be surprised to learn the law does not require a degree for someone to become a therapist or counselor, which is fine but you should know this up front. It is perfectly acceptable for you to sit down one on one and ask the counselor what exactly their level of experience is and to ask what methods they use or practice.

Psychotherapy cannot simply be learned out of a book or in a classroom. You want a therapist who has some experience under their belt and you feel comfortable with. Although, a psychologist may not necessarily be a better therapist than a licensed professional counselor; it's up to you to check out their credibility and beliefs carefully before beginning therapy.

Within a reasonable amount of time you should be making progress, however if you're not making progress, it might be time to re-evaluate some new goals. It's okay to ask questions and its okay to expect answers. Keep an open dialogue.

Your time is valuable and so is theirs', so be a respecter of time. Remember, there are no guarantees a therapist is responsible, informed, or even sane. It might be in your best interest to seek someone out who has a master's or a doctorate in a field of mental health (e.g., MA, MS, MSW, PhD, PsyD, MD).

David A. Reinstein, LCSW says it is important to find a good fit. While there are many extraordinary therapists out there; when you are in need of some counseling it is to your benefit to do a little research and ask a few questions. In essence, you are about to trust them with your utmost secrets.

Your therapist should be just this, "your" therapist not your buddy or your pall keep the relationship professional. Don't be afraid of a therapist who challenges you to take responsibility for your life, your choices, and your future. This is always better than one who teaches you to blame all problems on other people and your past. If you have one negative session I wouldn't suggest you terminate or switch therapists. One bad session is not an indication things are necessarily wrong.

A therapist's job is to help reduce suffering and increase the likelihood of healthy choice making. Beliefs, behaviors, or attitudes do not facilitate this goal, and are damaging to the likelihood of healing. David warns, "even after what seems to be a good beginning, there are some critical tell-tale signs the 'match' may not be the right one for you."

Here is a basic checklist of warning signs your therapeutic relationship might not be a good fit. These signs are listed on an article written by David Reinstein on Associated Content.

It's not a good fit if your therapist.........

1. "Forgets important information you have told them in recent sessions."
2. "Confuses their own experiences with those of yours."
3. "Becomes too reliant on a 'favorite' diagnosis, which seems to be the case more often than not with more clients than not."
4. "Believes when it comes to treatment, one particular intervention or technique is the right way to go with most clients most of the time."
5. "Seems to over identify with or take the side of one or another family member (most commonly found in couples and family therapy situations) and refuses to openly discuss the concerns; this perception/reality is generating in one or more of the other clients."
6. "Reacts to a client's questions, concerns, or criticisms defensively."
7. "Discusses work with other clients who are not directly involved in your therapy."
8. "Seems interested in and open to developing a personal relationship with you."
9. "Coaches, gives advice, or in other ways tries to actively lead you to a presumed 'correct' decision."
10. "Fails to identify the need for consultation for a particularly complex or challenging situation

and/or failing to recognize the need for the involvement of another discipline in the necessary treatment of a client."

11. "Does not listen."

12. "Believes (and communicates by words or attitude) the difference between themselves and you is more than education, role, and position in the relationship."

If it is not a good fit, you should discontinue therapy with this individual. If in doubt contact your personal physician to ask their expert opinion.

I want to remind those patients who have had a negative experience not to become discouraged. Don't give up if you fall into the hands of a therapist you do not feel is the correct fit. It is your prerogative to switch therapists if you are not feeling it is working. But, there are a few guidelines you should be aware of and if your therapist crosses the line then it is time to look for a new therapist. Those red flags are as follows.

1. Sexual relations of any kind are unacceptable between a therapist and a patient.

2. Your beliefs, religious, or political stance should be respected and never ridiculed.

3. A therapist should never make you feel disrespected and you should never be bullied into a response.

4. Remember, if it is not a good fit it is okay to acknowledge this, and to request a new therapist. If your therapist calls you once you have ceased this professional relationship, this is not acceptable.

Dr. Paul McHugh, Chair of the Psychiatry Department at Johns Hopkins University strongly suggests one should avoid any psychiatrists or therapists who engage in any 'memory recovery techniques'. Dr. McHugh, goes on to say "such 'memory recovery techniques' may include drug-mediated interviews, hypnosis, regression therapies, guided imagery, 'body memories', literal dream interpretation and journaling. There is no evidence the use of consciousness-altering techniques, such as drug-mediated interviews or hypnosis, can reveal or accurately elaborate factual information about any past experiences including childhood sexual abuse. Techniques of regression therapy including 'age regression' and hypnotic regression are of unproven effectiveness."

Dr. McHugh warns, "It is not known how to distinguish, with complete accuracy, memories based on true events from those derived from other sources. Memories can be significantly influenced by questioning, especially in young children. Memories also can be significantly influenced by a trusted person (e.g., therapist, parent involved in a custody dispute) who suggests abuse as an explanation for symptoms or problems, despite initial lack of memory of such abuse. It has also been shown repeated questioning may lead individuals to report "memories" of events, which never occurred."

If you have serious doubts about your current therapist or the therapy they are using, it is wise to get a second opinion from a responsible, licensed medical professional like your family doctor.

If there is unethical behavior you should file a complaint with a licensing board. Most importantly, if you did have or had a bad experience, this should not keep you from seeking help in the future.

Seeking wise counsel is a sign of maturity and humility. With this in mind it is important those who abuse their position as counselor must be exposed.

Chapter Nineteen
Getting back on your feet

"When all fails, the buck stops with YOU!"

Whatever your circumstance, decide to be better. If you feel you need therapy, find a good therapist. If you determine your relationship with your therapist is spinning its wheels, then find a new one. A good therapist will within a short time turn you lose to experience life and leave the door open for you to return.

This is what my therapist did to me. It has been six months and I have never been back. I am on no prescription drugs for depression or anxiety. Do I still feel the effects of my ordeal? You bet I do! Do I still hurt, is there still pain? You bet there is! Initially you may feel rejected by your therapist, but a good therapist or counselor will want you to become better.

I believe we were created to achieve great things. Those things are not outlined and defined by the world. They are defined by you. Determine within yourself to achieve, to be better. The key to it all is "you" are doing the deciding. If someone who has been abused is confiding in you, don't enforce your will upon them. Give input and advice if asked by the individual. I have had a number of good constituents in my life. The best ones were those who listened. People will spend a lot of hard earned money on motivational teachings. They are all good. The one aspect laced within the fabric of all of them is these principles.

The biggest lesson I have learned and have had to come to grips with is "it is what it is," there is nothing, absolutely nothing I can do to change what happened to me. I can therefore only determine where I will go in response to those circumstances I was forced to endure. I have decided to go on and make my mark on society.

The therapeutic relationship is one of the most "sacred" institutions in our culture today. This relationship can be with a clinical psychologist, licensed therapist or counselor, spiritual counselor such as a pastor or member of our church, or just a close friend. It is in this relationship we are encouraged to be vulnerable, to allow ourselves to feel emotions long buried and forgotten, and often times, relive some painful and violating past memories. In this relationship our choice of a therapist can often times be looked upon with the same trust a small child would place upon a parent, or an adult would place in a mentor/guide. She or he is the one who is counted upon to help us rebuild broken dreams, damaged hearts, and our shattered souls.

Yet, sometimes it is this very person who can violate us the most. When this happens, who do we look to for help, where do we turn, how do we learn we are not alone, and how do we heal? Do we go to the libraries and look up information about what has happened to us? We can, but odds are the library shelves will be barren.

Because therapy abuse is a "silent topic", one rarely talked about and often swept under the carpet. This is why you have to decide to better yourself. You will have to make hard decisions

about yourself. It all comes down to you. Go for
it, I know you can do it!

The Sierra Redwood by Michael Drummond

Chapter Twenty
Conclusion
By Pastor J. Frank Sinclair

As bizarre as the subject matter may appear and although the story sounds more science fiction than reality, let me assure you, it is true! How I know, you may ask; because I know the man. As I celebrate my 28th year as a Christian and 23rd as a pastor this year, there has never been a time during this period I didn't know Steve Skotko.

I still remember going into this brand new environment called Church and Steve welcoming me and being eager to show me the ropes. I am eternally grateful to this man whom God has used so instrumentally in my life, all glory to God!!!!

Steve was there when I met my wife, when our children were born, and when God was establishing His call in my heart. Steve was there encouraging us as we trod the often merciless path of ministry. When Steve was pastor of a small church in Butte, Montana, he introduced me to ministering to "the least of these" at Gospel missions. He allowed me to speak in his place. I continue this form of outreach to this day; speaking and encouraging the needy at the Colorado Springs Rescue Mission.

Steve is a Barnabas (encourager) to all of us who truly know him. Being true to what God made him to be, he now seeks to encourage a much maligned and hidden segment of Christianity, those who like himself have escaped spiritual abuse and anarchy.

When Steve first shared the depths of his story and pain with me, I was shocked. If I didn't know Steve personally, I admit, I would have probably dismissed his charges as being out of hand. My life's work is dealing with pain, in the lives of many and also in my own. God chooses to use the foolish to confound the wise.

The pain wrought by this unbiblical and outrageous repressed memory therapy is nothing short of demonic. Praise God He has chosen to expose this shadowy and dark process. Although Steve has reaped much pain from this practice, exposing lies is the responsibility of all Christians. We are commanded to not attack people (no biblical mandate), we are, however, to hold them responsible for their fruit.

Steve seeks to do just this. Many of us lack this courage; this is unfortunate, since our God is strong!! Steve demonstrated true courage in writing this book and having a willingness to endure the backlash both inside and outside of the Christian community.

Mostly though, he has had to endure the "dark days of the soul" and the sometimes unbearable pain of his own heart in walking through this. Please don't patronize him with the phrase "I know how you are feeling brother" sentiment. We don't know. Simply open your minds and hearts to the depths the enemy will go to destroy a life and remember he will do whatever it takes to destroy yours as well. Read and heed the Lord's voice as He sounds the alarm to another of the devil's schemes.

357

Bravo Steve, well done!!!!!

In Him
J. Frank Sinclair
Associate Pastor; The Grace Place Church
Colorado Springs, Colorado.

This book is based upon actual events, court document of the case, emails and personal testimonies have been added to prove the credibility of Steve's story. Steve was found innocent of all charges and has filed suit against Marion Knox. The views expressed are from Steve's perspective and from his experience. Information has been gathered from a variety of sources. Those sources are presumed to be true.

If you feel you have suffered abuse in any fashion please contact your local authorities or call your local help line.

Please feel free to contact us at the following email address: www.helpforvictims@yahoo.com. We are here to help and offer you support.

Stephan is currently a student finishing his Bachelor's degree in healthcare administration. He resides in Seven Hills, Ohio.